ANIME

by Hal Marcovitz

LUCENT BOOKS

An imprint of Thomson Gale, a part of The Thomson Corporation

THOMSON

GALE

Detroit • New York • San Francisco • New Haven, Conn. • Waterville, Maine • London

THOMSON

™

GALE

LIBRARY OF CONGRESS CATALOGING-IN-PUBLICATION DATA

Marcovitz, Hal.
  Anime / by Hal Marcovitz.
     p. cm. — (Eye on art)
  Includes bibliographical references and index.
  ISBN-13: 978-1-59018-995-5 (hardcover)
  1. Animated films—Japan—Juvenile literature. I. Title.
  NC1766.J3M28 2008
  791.43'340952—dc22

                                                                    2007023008

ISBN-10: 1-59018-995-7
Printed in the United States of America

CONTENTS

96,679

Foreword

"Art has no other purpose than to brush aside . . . everything that veils reality from us in order to bring us face to face with reality itself."
—French philosopher Henri-Louis Bergson

Some thirty-one thousand years ago, early humans painted strikingly sophisticated images of horses, bison, rhinoceroses, bears, and other animals on the walls of a cave in southern France. The meaning of these elaborate pictures is unknown, although some experts speculate that they held ceremonial significance. Regardless of their intended purpose, the Chauvet-Pont-d'Arc cave paintings represent some of the first known expressions of the artistic impulse.

From the Paleolithic era to the present day, human beings have continued to create works of visual art. Artists have developed painting, drawing, sculpture, engraving, and many other techniques to produce visual representations of landscapes, the human form, religious and historical events, and countless other subjects. The artistic impulse also finds expression in glass, jewelry, and new forms inspired by new technology. Indeed, judging by humanity's prolific artistic output throughout history, one must conclude that the compulsion to produce art is an inherent aspect of being human, and the results are among humanity's greatest cultural achievements: masterpieces such as the architectural marvels of ancient Greece, Michelangelo's perfectly rendered statue *David*, Vincent van Gogh's visionary painting *Starry Night*, and endless other treasures.

The creative impulse serves many purposes for society. At its most basic level, art is a form of entertainment or the means for a satisfying or pleasant aesthetic experience. But art's true power lies not in its potential to entertain and delight but in its ability to enlighten, to reveal the truth, and by doing so to uplift the human spirit and transform the human race.

One of the primary functions of art has been to serve religion. For most of Western history, for example, artists were paid by the church to produce works with religious themes and subjects. Art was thus a tool to help human beings transcend mundane, secular reality and achieve spiritual enlightenment. One of the best-known, and largest-scale, examples of Christian religious art is the Sistine Chapel in the Vatican in Rome. In 1508 Pope Julius II commissioned Italian Renaissance artist Michelangelo to paint the chapel's vaulted ceiling, an area of 640 square yards (535 sq. m). Michelangelo spent four years on scaffolding, his neck craned, creating a panoramic fresco of some three hundred human figures. His paintings depict Old Testament prophets and heroes, sibyls of Greek mythology, and nine scenes from the Book of Genesis, including the Creation of Adam, the Fall of Adam and Eve from the Garden of Eden, and the Flood. The ceiling of the Sistine Chapel is considered one of the greatest works of Western art and has inspired the awe of countless Christian pilgrims and other religious seekers. As eighteenth-century German poet and author Johann Wolfgang von Goethe wrote, "Until you have seen this Sistine Chapel, you can have no adequate conception of what man is capable of."

In addition to inspiring religious fervor, art can serve as a force for social change. Artists are among the visionaries of any culture. As such, they often perceive injustice and wrongdoing and confront others by reflecting what they see in their work. One classic example of art as social commentary was created in May 1937, during the brutal Spanish civil war. On May 1 Spanish artist Pablo Picasso learned of the recent attack on the small Basque village of Guernica by German airplanes allied with fascist forces led by Francisco Franco. The German pilots had used the village for target practice, a three-hour bombing that killed sixteen hundred civilians. Picasso, living in Paris, channeled his outrage over the massacre into his painting *Guernica,* a black, white, and gray mural that depicts dismembered animals and fractured human figures whose faces are contorted in agonized expressions. Initially, critics and the public condemned the painting as an incoherent hodgepodge, but the work soon came to be seen as a powerful antiwar statement and remains an iconic symbol of the violence and terror that dominated world events during the remainder of the twentieth century.

The impulse to create art—whether painting animals with crude pigments on a cave wall, sculpting a human form from marble, or commemorating human tragedy in a mural—thus serves many purposes. It offers an entertaining diversion, nourishes the imagination and the spirit, decorates and beautifies the world, and chronicles the age. But underlying all these functions is the desire to reveal that which is obscure—to illuminate, clarify, and perhaps ennoble. As Picasso himself stated, "The purpose of art is washing the dust of daily life off our souls."

The Eye on Art series is intended to assist readers in understanding the various roles of art in society. Each volume offers an in-depth exploration of a major artistic movement, medium, figure, or profession. All books in the series are beautifully illustrated with full-color photographs and diagrams. Riveting narrative, clear technical explanation, informative sidebars, fully documented quotes, a bibliography, and a thorough index all provide excellent starting points for research and discussion. With these features, the Eye on Art series is a useful introduction to the world of art—a world that can offer both insight and inspiration.

Introduction

Anime: A Gift from Japan

A spaceship glides across the screen. Tension builds as the hollow, rhythmic sounds of a wooden drum resonate in an ever-increasing tempo. Inside the craft, the plucky heroine barks out orders to her crewmates. She is tall and sure of herself; viewers cannot help but notice her childlike face, wild and unruly hair, wide round eyes, and costume showing off her long and slender legs. Soon she will battle the evil scourge of the galaxy; in this film, though, there is no guarantee she will win. In fact, she might not even survive the adventure.

Thus is the world of anime (pronounced annie-MAY), the enormously popular form of Japanese animation that has captured a significant audience of filmgoers in America and other countries as well. Anime fans can find new titles churned out constantly by animation studios in Japan, where it has become a $5 billion a year industry. Anime can be seen on broadcast and cable TV, found in theaters, and is available for home viewing on the Internet as well as in DVD and VHS formats. When not watching anime, fans can sit down with Japanese-produced graphic novels known as manga (pronounced mang-AH). Publishers print hundreds of titles a year.

What Is Anime?

Anime has been produced in Japan for nearly a century. There is no Japanese word for animation, so the early Japanese animators borrowed the French term *animé* and incorporated it into their language. Manga is a Japanese word that translates into "random pictures." Manga is the genre of graphic novels and comic books that essentially tell the same stories on the printed page that anime tells on the screen. Early anime was often based on characters and stories that initially appeared in manga. Even today, much of anime is adapted from manga, just as many American-made films are adapted from novels and similar sources.

The anime that Americans see in the theaters or on TV in their homes is a fraction of what is produced in Japan. Most of the anime available in America features adventure or science

The uniquely Japanese art form of anime has developed a large following worldwide.

fiction stories, but in Japan anime is used by filmmakers to tell a variety of stories, including romances, mysteries, historical dramas, slapstick comedies, and fairy tales. Said writer Shinobu Price, "The only thing that really classifies anime as, well, anime is the fact that it is made in Japan by Japanese artists within a Japanese context. Stylistic experimentation with the medium is expected—rewarded if it's good. . . . The creative realm of anime is vast, the possibilities endless."[1]

In America, anime is regarded as an art form appreciated mostly by teenagers—although there are exceptions, such as the Pokémon video games, films, and TV shows that appeal to young children. Nevertheless, in Japan the fan base is far wider. Audiences range from very young children to adults.

A manga comic book cover shows the wide, round eyes and wild hair that are classic features of anime.

There is a similar audience for manga. In America manga can be found on the shelves of most bookstores. Many libraries that have created graphic novel sections are sure to include manga titles among the selections. As with anime, though, manga is far more widespread in Japan than in America. In Japan, manga titles account for nearly a third of all books and magazines published in the country.

Some Americans grew up watching anime without realizing it. In the 1960s the first Japanese anime stories started appearing on American TV with the broadcasts of such shows as *Astro Boy*, *Kimba the White Lion*, and *Speed Racer*. The TV shows were dubbed into English and edited so that most of the Japanese content was taken out—for example, a scene in which the characters dine with chopsticks was typically cut out of the American version. Usually, the only hint that the shows originated in Japan came at the end when the credits rolled by, giving the young viewers reason to wonder why all the creative people involved in the production of the shows seemed to have Japanese names.

Anime Explosion

Beginning in the late 1970s the anime explosion hit American pop culture. Thanks to the development of videocassette players, Americans could watch the original anime shows as they were produced in Japan. At first, tourists brought the tapes home and shared them with friends. Soon video rental stores featured anime shelves. The appeal of anime initially spread through word of mouth but it did not take long for American studios, TV networks, and publishers to get the message about anime and manga.

As for what was going on up there on the screen, Americans who were used to seeing the state-of-the-art animation produced by the Walt Disney studio for such films as *The Little Mermaid* and *Aladdin* saw far different stories unfold in Japanese anime. In the Disney films young heroes and heroines overcome great odds to defeat the villains, find love, and live happily ever after. In Japanese anime the stories are often far darker, the motives of the heroes not always righteous, the villains often misunderstood,

A fan reads a typical Japanese manga comic book illustrated with black and white line drawings.

and seldom does anybody seem to live happily ever after. According to Price, these types of characteristics found in anime stories are largely responsible for attracting a huge audience to the genre. She said,

> This uniquely odd world of Japanese animation may be the very reason why it appeals to so many outsiders. The way anime uses its medium of animation is so fundamentally different from the artistic tradition of Walt Disney, that it creates a freshly intriguing aroma that lures foreigners into its mist. . . . The fact that death can strike at any time to any character may indeed be a culturally significant characteristic, but it also makes for one hell of a plot twist. This gives anime a rather exotic charm. [2]

What is more, anime has attracted a large audience even though the animation has often been well behind the artistic quality of the Disney films or even the shows broadcast on Saturday morning children's television. With smaller budgets with which to work, Japanese animators produced a rougher and more static form of animated art. And manga has always seemed a step below the standards of American-produced comic art. Most manga is rendered in black and white line drawings, a quality that is far below what Americans are used to reading. Imagine following the exploits of Superman in black and white: no red and blue costume, no red kryptonite to endanger him, no orange hair atop the head of Jimmy Olsen, no lively urban colors punctuating the city of Metropolis. And yet, despite the clear drop-off in quality the appeal of the stories cannot be denied, which has helped manga as well as anime capture a truly dedicated audience of fans in America.

1

The Roots of Anime

In Japan there is a long tradition of storytelling through pictures that dates back at least to the twelfth century, when artists illustrated a story titled *Tale of Genji*. Written some one hundred years before by Murasaki Shikibu, a lady-in-waiting to the Japanese empress Akiko, *Tale of Genji* is believed to be history's first novel. It relates the adventures of Prince Genji, a noble warrior and romantic figure. *Tale of Genji* is one of Japan's most important works of literature, and nearly one thousand years after it was written, the book remains in publication today.

In its original version readers followed the fifty-four-chapter story by unrolling a scroll. The words were laid out in a vertical format and read right to left—which is how Japanese is still read today. In the twelfth century Japanese artists started producing what is known as *emakimono*—an illustrated scroll told through words and pictures laid out in a horizontal format. *Tale of Genji* was the first example of emakimono. By now, other artists were drawing what became known as *giga*, which means "funny pictures." In giga, the stories were shorter than what readers could find in emakimono. Modern manga and its offspring, anime, have their roots in giga and emakimono. As for manga, that term was first applied to a series of sketches drawn by a Japanese artist named Katsushika Hokusai in the early nineteenth century.

Although modern manga and anime are unique forms of Japanese art, they both owe their explosive growth to Western influences. It took the opening of trade routes to show the Japanese the enormous potential of their own comic art.

Murasaki Shikibu, pictured at work in this illustration, wrote one of Japan's most important works of literature, *Tale of Genji.*

Feudal Past

By the nineteenth century Europeans and Americans had started making their way to Japan. Trade between Japan and the Western world commenced, particularly after Commodore Matthew Perry signed a treaty with Japan in 1854, establishing diplomatic relations between the United States and the Asian nation. The Japanese soon became dedicated readers of newspapers and magazines published in Europe and America that arrived aboard ships docking in Tokyo and other cities. Japanese readers

TWO INFLUENTIAL EUROPEANS

In the 1860s two Europeans arrived in Japan and would soon become influential figures in the development of Japanese comic art. Charles Wirgman, a British journalist, established a publication he titled *Japan Punch*, which was styled after the British version of the magazine that had been published in London for some twenty years. *Japan Punch* featured comic strips, which the Japanese called "ponchi," a word based on the title of the publication. Meanwhile, a competing publication, *Tobae*, was established by a French painter living in Japan, George Bigot. The title of the publication was drawn from the name of twelfth-century emakimono artist Sojo Toba.

Japan Punch and *Tobae* introduced formats still used in comic book art today—dialogue was lettered into balloons above the heads of the characters, and the stories were presented in panels that followed one another in sequence. "The Japanese were fortunate to have Wirgman and Bigot as mentors," said Frederik L. Schodt. "Both men were not only excellent cartoonists but accomplished formal artists from whom European advances in perspective, anatomy and shading (things Japanese artists had not always put fully to use) could be studied."

Frederik L. Schodt, *Manga! Manga! The World of Japanese Comics.* Tokyo: Kodansha International, 1986, p. 40.

were particularly fond of *Punch* and *Puck*, the satirical British magazines that told most of their stories in cartoons.

By the late 1800s Japanese versions of *Punch* and *Puck* as well as many other digests of cartoon art had been established in Tokyo and other Japanese cities. Among the top artists of the era were Ippei Okamoto and Rakuten Kitazawa. Born in 1876, Kitazawa became a newspaper cartoonist in Japan; his most popular cartoon told of the ongoing comic antics of Donsha, a street waif. He also helped found *Tokyo Puck*, the Japanese version of the British satire magazine.

Okamoto, who was born in 1886, helped organize Japanese comic artists into a professional association known as Nippon Mangakai. Okamoto was well traveled. He visited the United States shortly after alcohol was banned by Prohibition, and reported back to his countrymen that Americans had found comfort in the Sunday comics. He wrote, "The American people love to laugh, but not in the stiff manner of the British. Their laugh is an innocent one that instantly dispels fatigue. . . . American comics have become an entertainment equal to baseball, motion pictures and the presidential elections. Some observers say that comics have replaced alcohol as a solace for workers since Prohibition began."[3]

Kitazawa, Okamoto, and their contemporaries were responsible for introducing some innovations that are still found in comic art today—dialogue was lettered into balloons above the heads of the characters, and the stories were presented in panels that followed one another in sequence. Meanwhile, artists were working in other mediums. In 1917 a twenty-nine-year-old amateur filmmaker named Oten Shimokawa, a former editorial assistant at *Tokyo Puck*, produced a five-minute animated cartoon. Shimokawa produced the cartoon, titled *Mukuzo Imokawa, The Doorkeeper*, by drawing the images right onto the film. (A first effort, in which he photographed drawings made by chalk on blackboard, did not translate well to film.) *Mukuzo*

Japanese artists introduced the use of dialogue balloons commonly found in modern comic art.

Imokawa, The Doorkeeper is regarded as the first anime film. A year later another animator, Jun-ichi Kouchi, produced a short cartoon about a little boy named Momotaro who protected Japan by patrolling Tokyo harbor in his toy submarine. In the years to come, Momotaro—also known as the "Peach Boy"—would evolve into a familiar folk hero to the Japanese people, becoming their version of Superman.

Preparing for War

The images drawn by the early animators were crude, to be sure, and over the next few years Japanese animation remained a hardscrabble form of art as animators experimented with a number of different processes to make their pictures move on the screen. In 1928, when Walt Disney unveiled *Steamboat Willie,* showing a crisply drawn Mickey Mouse navigating over a choppy river, Japanese artists were still experimenting with animating characters they cut out of paper. Still, Japanese animation was fun to watch. Animators used the crude medium to tell stories about animals causing mischief and plucky children outwitting oafish adults. Japanese folktales were also brought to life in these early examples of anime.

That would soon change. By the 1930s a military regime was in control of the country. As Japan prepared for war, the government encouraged animators to portray the exploits of heroes performing deeds to save the nation from foreign aggressors. In 1931 Momotaro reappeared, only now he was leading the Japanese navy into battle against all manner of cartoon villains. Momotaro and the navy always won. In one chilling anime film, produced in 1933 and titled *Black Cat Banzai,* Momotaro repels an invasion of bombers flown by an army of rodents who closely resembled Mickey Mouse. (Of course, more than a decade later, it would take more than Momotaro to protect Japan from an invading force of American bombers, and this time Mickey Mouse would not be at the controls.) Nevertheless, after Japan invaded China in 1937 all films, including anime, had to be approved by government censors. Only those films containing a strong message of propaganda and designed to lift the spirits of the population were approved.

Following the Japanese attack on Pearl Harbor in 1941, the regime stepped up calls for propaganda films, but Japanese animators were hampered by the war economy. By now Japanese animators were making films the same way animators made them elsewhere: The images were drawn on translucent cels, which were placed against a nonmoving background and photographed cel by cel with movie film. The cels are made out of cellulose, which is the substance that gives plants their structure. But cellulose is a key ingredient in weapons making, and that is what most of Japan's cellulose supply was used for during the war. As a result, much of the anime produced during World War II has been destroyed. To save cels, animators would use the cellulose sheets, then wash off the images so they could be reinked. Still, a lot of

The gallant cartoon character Momotaro, honored with a statue, had many guises, but he always protected Japan from invaders.

anime was produced during the war, and much of it was made with money provided by the military. Many anime films featured Momotaro, who was still protecting Japan from invaders.

Still, as the war dragged on and it became increasingly clear to Japanese leaders that they were going to lose, they stepped up calls for animation to prop up the spirits of the people. In April 1945, at a time when the Japanese Imperial Navy was otherwise preoccupied with preparing for an anticipated Allied invasion of the island, its admirals still found the resources to finance one last Momotaro adventure. The film, titled *Momotaro's Divine Sea Warriors*, was the first feature-length anime movie produced in Japan. The film depicts the Peach Boy leading a band of monkeys, rabbits, and other cute critters into an air strike that repels a British invasion force. At the end of the film Momotaro parachutes onto a map of the United States—perhaps whetting the appetite of the audience for a sequel, which was never made.

Manga Pioneer

After Japan's defeat in 1945 the animation and publishing industries—as with most of the rest of the Japanese economy—were in shambles. At the end of the war the Americans and British arrived to install a democratic government, rebuild Japanese infrastructure and industry, and find jobs for millions of unemployed workers. Reestablishing the anime and manga industries was not a top priority for the officials in charge of Japanese reconstruction. For the first few years following the war few theaters were in operation, and they showed mostly American and British films made available to audiences by the occupying armies. Essentially, there was no new anime produced and hardly any manga available. Rarely could readers afford to buy manga anyway, but something of a "manga rental" industry grew up after the war. Instead of selling the books, bookstores rented the titles to readers. Said author and anime expert Gilles Poitras,

> The decade after the war was a hard one for both anime and cinema due to the great damage inflicted upon the country. Many theaters and production venues had been destroyed. All the same, the manga industry grew as a

THE WALT DISNEY OF JAPAN

Osamu Tezuka is often referred to as the "Walt Disney of Japan." Just as Disney helped launch the animation industry in the United States, Tezuka is given credit as the most influential anime and manga artist in Japan.

Born in 1928, Tezuka entered medical school shortly after World War II. He obtained a medical degree, but by then he was already a busy manga artist. He soon dropped his medical career to concentrate on manga.

Before he turned his attention to developing anime in the early 1960s, Tezuka produced a stunning amount of manga. It is believed he wrote and illustrated more than seven hundred volumes of manga that included some 170,000 pages.

Although he won fame as the creator of Mighty Atom and other heroic figures, Tezuka drew manga in many genres. One of his most successful series of manga novels includes the *Phoenix* stories, historical manga novels set in eighth-century Japan that follow a holy man and a gifted artist through many trials that test their faith and goodness.

Tezuka died in 1989, a victim of stomach cancer. The anime studio he founded, Mushi Productions, remains in business today and actively produces animated films. Many of the characters he created are constantly given new life by Japanese toy companies or featured in new productions of Tezuka's original stories.

cheap form of entertainment that did not require buildings and projectors; one could easily rent manga from special shops, predecessors to video stores.[4]

Indeed, out of the rubble of World War II grew the foundations of today's anime and manga industries, and it was due mostly to the efforts of a single artist. Osamu Tezuka entered medical

Osamu Tezuka created thought-provoking stories with manga. Pictured is a scene from *Metropolis,* a movie based on one of his stories.

school shortly after the war but soon gave up the practice of medicine to concentrate on his passion—comic art. Tezuka was very influenced by Disney animation—he had been awestruck by the Disney studio's 1942 animated film *Bambi,* which played in Japanese theaters after the war. (In 1951 he received permission from Disney to produce a manga version of *Bambi* for Japanese readers.)

As the publishing industry slowly recovered, publishers needed qualified artists to produce manga titles. Tezuka soon became a busy artist, providing illustrations for a number of Japanese publications, including children's picture books, adventure stories for teens, and detective stories for adults. In 1947 Tezuka wrote and illustrated a two-hundred-page graphic novel titled *New Treasure Island*, which is regarded as the first modern work of manga. Japanese readers embraced the title, buying some 400,000 copies. In producing *New Treasure Island* and other titles, Tezuka essentially used anime techniques to tell a story in a printed format. He changed viewpoints often—in one frame showing a character from afar and in the next, illustrating the character in an extreme close-up. Tezuka also developed the technique still employed today by manga and anime artists of using his characters' facial expressions—as much as dialogue—to tell the story. Said American author and anime authority Frederik L. Schodt,

> Tezuka was a real pioneer. He was trying to use the comic book medium to tell stories. He was one of the first people who seriously tried to use manga in this way, just as film directors use film or novelists use novels. As a result, his stories are very thought-provoking. There's always something that children can enjoy, but actually adults can enjoy them too because they have many layers of meaning. There is a superficial layer which is just entertainment, but there is often a very philosophical layer, just like in a good movie or novel.[5]

Tetsuan Atom

During the 1950s Tezuka expanded manga into many genres, finding audiences from very young children to adults. In Japan the first readers of manga were teenagers. As they grew older, Tezuka developed titles in romance, mystery, drama, and other adult-oriented fiction to keep them reading manga as adults. He also produced manga for young children, usually featuring cute and magical animal characters in fairy tale–style adventures.

Meanwhile, during the 1950s, independent animators found a way to restart the industry that had virtually disappeared after Momotaro's last adventure in the waning days of the war. Like

Tezuka, the Japanese artists working in anime were very influenced by the films of the Disney studio, and they concentrated on stories featuring old Japanese folk tales. In 1960 Tezuka agreed to permit a group of independent artists to animate one of his manga stories, *Alakazam the Great*. The manga book and its subsequent film told the story of a young monkey king who challenges the gods and is then sent back to Earth to learn humility and serve as the bodyguard for a prince. Tezuka quickly realized the potential of the new genre. Mostly Tezuka believed that Japanese audiences would welcome fast-paced adventure stories featuring heroic characters. With television growing as a medi-

MANGA CAFÉS

Manga is so popular in Japan that entrepreneurs have established manga cafés and manga libraries. These are places where fans can read manga while they eat, drink coffee, and discuss the latest titles with other readers. It is estimated that there are some three hundred manga cafés and libraries in Tokyo alone.

Some manga cafés stock as many as thirty thousand titles on their shelves. At a manga café customers order food or coffee and relax while they read through the latest manga titles. A manga library is not like the typical public library found in America. Since the manga libraries do not sell food or drinks, customers are charged an hourly fee to read the manga on the libraries' shelves. Library customers are free to bring their own food and beverages, though.

Manga cafés and libraries are found in most Japanese cities. Some cities have also established museums dedicated to popular manga artists and their work. A museum dedicated to the work of early manga artist Rakuten Kitazawa has been established in the city of Omiya. The city of Takarazuka, where *Mighty Atom* creator Osamu Tezuka lived as a boy, has created a museum dedicated to the work of the pioneering manga and anime artist.

um of entertainment in Japan, Tezuka decided to concentrate on producing content for Japanese TV rather than theatrical release. In 1961 he created Japan's first animation studio—Mushi Productions. Mushi's first show was titled *Tetsuan Atom*—in English, *Mighty Atom*—which was based on one of Tezuka's manga titles from 1953. The show told the story of a robot boy created by a grieving scientist as a replacement for his dead son. It was more or less a science-fictional retelling of *Pinocchio*.

Along with the action as well as its good-versus-evil scenario, Tezuka ensured that *Tetsuan Atom* would include strong characters who showed human emotions and concerns. Tezuka found that he could constantly refine the characters as the story progressed from week to week. Of course, there was a strong dose of science fiction served up to the viewers as well: Atom, a true superhero, could speak sixty languages and fly by converting his feet into jet engines. He also possessed super strength, super vision, and super hearing and could shoot lasers out of his hips. His heart could detect people's evil intentions. Eventually, Tezuka

Alakazam the Great was another of Osamu Tezuka's stories that became a movie.

provided Atom with a robot sister and an evil twin brother. *Tetsuan Atom* soon became enormously popular in Japan. Each week an estimated 40 percent of all households in Japan tuned in to watch the robot boy's next adventure. Wrote American anime authority Fred Patten,

> It was an instant success, completely transforming animation in Japan, by showing there was a vast public demand for comic book–style action-adventure in modern or futuristic settings. It also showed that the public would accept TV-quality animation; limited but fast-paced. This effectively put the individual artist-animators out of business, since they could not produce cartoons fast enough for the TV market, but enabled several fledgling animators to get the financial backing to start their own studios.[6]

Tetsuan Atom premiered on Japanese TV in 1963 and would remain a staple of Japanese anime for three years. Nearly 200 episodes were aired. A few months after its debut on Japanese TV, an American TV producer imported the series, had it dubbed into English, and changed the name to *Astro Boy*. Japanese anime had now arrived in America.

Anime in America

By modern standards *Astro Boy* would hardly qualify as groundbreaking animation. The show was broadcast in black and white, and the animation was well below the quality of shows that American children could see elsewhere on TV—shows such as *The Flintstones, Bugs Bunny, The Bullwinkle Show,* and *Huckleberry Hound.* What is more, to fit into an American TV format, *Astro Boy* had to be heavily edited, which often made each week's plot confusing.

Still, *Astro Boy* was the first show in what would soon become a tidal wave of Japanese animation—often called Japanimation by Americans—that would hit the airwaves in the United States. Soon other shows would follow, and over the next several years the animation quality and content of Japanese-produced shows improved.

Meanwhile, in America, anime developed a cultlike following as teenagers and other fans, starved for science fiction, adventure, and fantasy entertainment, found a deep source for those genres in the vast library of anime and manga that was produced in Japan. Said Patten, "*Astro Boy* proved that a Japanese animated series could be successful in North America, paving the way for all that followed."[7]

Edited for U.S. television and re-titled *Astro Boy,* Tezuka's popular Japanese series about a boy robot marked anime's arrival in America.

Producing a Pilot

When *Tetsuan Atom* premiered on Japanese TV it was inked and broadcast in black and white, because Tezuka's studio did not have the budget to produce a color cartoon, nor did the Fuji Television Network own the equipment to broadcast in color. Besides, in the early 1960s, there were few color TVs in Japan, anyway.

Nevertheless, when an NBC television network executive who was based in Japan turned on his TV and saw an episode featuring the exploits of the brave little rocket boy, he thought it might have potential in America. The executive obtained some copies of the show from Fuji and shipped them back to NBC in New York. After receiving the shows, the network got in touch with Fred Ladd.

Ladd was an independent television producer who specialized in taking documentaries about wildlife filmed in Europe and editing them for broadcast on American TV. Frequently, the documentaries spanned between 30 and 50 minutes, meaning they could not fit into the 30- and 60-minute time slots networks demand for their shows. Ladd reedited the European documentaries into lengths that could be shown on American TV. He also had the narrations dubbed into English.

Ladd also had some experience in animation. He helped produce English-language versions of several European cartoons, including the movie-length Belgian animation, *Pinocchio in Outer Space*, which he recut and dubbed into English for American audiences.

Ladd was approached by NBC to look over some episodes of *Tetsuan Atom* to see whether it could be packaged for audiences in the United States. Ladd immediately recognized the show's potential. He edited one of the episodes into a pilot, which is a trial version of a show that is tested in front of an audience. He said,

> Sometime in 1963, NBC's representative in Tokyo saw a very, very limited action, adventure show on television about a little boy called *Tetsuan Atom*. . . . NBC Enterprises, a division of the broadcast network, picked it up very cheap, not even knowing what they were buying. No one spoke Japanese. No one really understood it.

They then tracked me down, knowing I had done a lot of cartoon dubbing as well as *Pinocchio in Outer Space,* and showed me a couple of episodes and asked me what I thought. As a result, I made a pilot, NBC saw it and said, "All right, do another one. We can sell this." I did and it became *Astro Boy.*[8]

Lacking in Quality

NBC could not keep the translated name *Mighty Atom*—there was already a comic book hero in the United States by that name. So Ladd changed his name to *Astro Boy.* This was the era in which the first American astronauts were being launched into space, and Ladd knew that a lot of public interest was already being shown in anything that sounded as though it involved adventures in space.

Instead of airing the show on NBC, network executives elected instead to "syndicate" the program, meaning they sold it station by station to their affiliates as well as to independent TV stations. Still, *Astro Boy* was aired in most major TV markets in the United States, and it proved to be popular among its young viewers. American producers soon imported more Mushi shows, including *Kimba the White Lion*, which featured the adventures of a young lion in Africa who protected the animals of his homeland; *Gigantor*, a story about a young boy's friendship with a giant crime-fighting robot; *Speed Racer*, which featured the

Astro Boy appealed to young American television viewers, prompting a new wave of animated series from Japan.

KIMBA AND *THE LION KING*

Soon after the Disney studio released *The Lion King* in 1994, anime fans discovered many similarities between the Disney animated film and the old Japanese TV series, *Kimba the White Lion*. For starters, the names of the two main characters were quite similar. In the old TV series Kimba was the main character; in the Disney film the young lion cub destined to be king is named Simba.

The plots were similar as well. Kimba was robbed of his title by an evil lion. So was Simba. In the TV series Kimba was helped by a wise old baboon and a talking bird. Similar characters befriended Simba. Said Fred Ladd, the American producer who edited *Kimba* for American audiences, "There are inescapable comparisons."

Executives from the Disney studio denied that they had borrowed liberally from the old *Kimba* show—a situation that could expose the studio to expensive lawsuits. *Kimba*'s originator, Osamu Tezuka, died before *The Lion King* was released, but American anime authority Frederik L. Schodt said Tezuka would not be offended if he had known Disney borrowed elements from his story. "He would be chuckling," Schodt said. "He might find it flattering."

Quoted in Ann Oldenburg, "The Lion King Shares a Jungle Crown," *USA Today*, July 14, 1994, p. D-1.

exploits of a race car driver who frequently found himself caught up in intrigue involving spies, evil scientists, and assorted other thugs; and *8 Man*, a series about a murdered detective given new life as a robot. (He went under the name of "Tobor"—*robot* spelled backward.)

Despite the appeal of the early shows, anime would hardly take over American TV. For starters, there was a clear drop-off in quality between the Japanese shows and the American-made

American-made cartoons such as those featuring *Bugs Bunny* exhibited a higher quality of animation than most of the shows coming out of Japan.

King Arth-Hare's Court

animated shows such as *The Flintstones* and *Bugs Bunny*, as well as the films produced by the Disney studio. Starting with *Kimba*, the Japanese shows were animated in color but obviously produced on tight budgets. To save money, artists used fewer animation cels. As such, anime often lacked the quality of American animation. In some scenes it seemed as though the only parts of the character that were truly animated were the eyes and the mouth—the rest of the body stood rock-still against the equally stagnant background.

Also, the Japanese programs were heavily edited. In addition to the English dubbing, the editors Americanized the characters' names and chopped out most references to Japanese culture—such as when characters ate with chopsticks, consumed the Japanese rice wine known as sake, or bowed to one another in greeting. What is more, American animators had fallen under strict guidelines when it came to portraying violence in children's programming. There were no such rules in Japan, and as a result, anime often featured extremely violent acts. Those scenes were cut out of the American versions, which satisfied network censors but usually affected the story lines and made the plots choppy or hard to follow. Finally, in Japan the stories were usually told as serials—each show was based on events and plot twists told in the previous week's show. In America the shows were edited so that the story could be related in a single episode.

Space Battleship Yamato

While anime settled into a niche in American entertainment reserved for children, back in Japan the animation industry had exploded. Unlike America, where animated shows had always been regarded as programming intended strictly for young children, in Japan teenagers and adults were also avid fans. Tezuka's Mushi Productions developed shows for older viewers, often adapting classical stories to anime. For example, Mushi produced anime versions of the Arabian series of folktales, *A Thousand and One Nights*, as well as *Cleopatra*, a story about the doomed Egyptian queen. Also, Mushi and its many competitors—since the early 1960s dozens of new animation studios had opened in Japan—were now producing sophisticated science fiction and adventure dramas. In 1974 Japanese audiences had their first look at a TV series titled *Space Battleship Yamato*, in which an old World War II battleship, the *Yamato*, is converted into a spaceship which travels the galaxy searching for an anti-radiation device that will save Earth.

The design of the futuristic Tokyo water-bus *Himiko* (pictured) may have been influenced by the television series *Space Battleship Yamato*.

Space Battleship Yamato featured sophisticated scripts that were several steps beyond the simple stories of good versus evil that children could see on *Astro Boy* or *Speed Racer*. For example, the show resurrected the Japanese people's uncomfortable memories of World War II, suggesting that a weapon from the old Japanese Imperial Navy, the *Yamato*, could now be used to save Earth. In addition to the thought-provoking scripts, *Space Battleship Yamato* featured strong character development and a high quality of animation. Said American anime authorities Jonathan Clements and Helen McCarthy,

> *Space Battleship Yamato* [*SBY*] is one of the watersheds in anime history . . . [the show] contained a supremely strong story line. *SBY* changed the way TV programmers thought about science fiction; previously, it had been supposed that only very young audiences watched TV anime, and so there was no point in screening anything but giant-robot and [superhero] shows. The influence of the original series on a whole generation of Japanese animators is incredible. [9]

Soon other animated space dramas went into production. Among the shows that debuted on Japanese TV during this era were *Mazinger Z*, a series about the adventures of a flying mechanical warrior; *Captain Harlock*, which told of a pirate who did his buccaneering in a space ship; and *Queen Millennia*, which related the story of an extraterrestrial queen who protected Earth from evil forces on her home planet.

Thought-Provoking Plots

At first, *Space Battleship Yamato* as well as the other animated science fiction shows were not broadcast on American TV. In fact, American audiences had no idea that anime had progressed beyond the quality of *Kimba the White Lion*—which during the 1970s was still being broadcast on American TV. But things started changing in the late 1970s, thanks mostly to the development of the videocassette player.

Tapes of original Japanese anime started making their way into American markets. Some of the tapes were brought home by tourists, but other tapes were being stocked on "anime shelves" in videotape rental stores or were bought and sold at science fiction conventions. Even though the dialogue was in Japanese, many dedicated anime fans were able to follow the stories despite the language barrier.

What is more, American fans discovered that anime was not just for kids. In a culture that was suddenly smitten by science fiction—the first *Star Wars* film had premiered in 1977, ushering in

The animated space dramas so popular in Japan reached a new level with the American-made *Star Wars* movies, featuring characters such as C-3PO (left), shown on the set of the first *Star Wars* film.

a new era in science fiction entertainment—American fans discovered that anime was dominated by space adventures, many told on a teenage or adult level featuring romance, violence, and plots in which the lines between good and evil were often blurred.

Of course, American TV producers soon got wind of the popularity of Japanese animation and started obtaining anime for broadcast in the American market. Among the first of the new breed of anime shows to be featured on TV was *Battle of the Planets*. The show, which debuted in 1978, told the story of five young heroes and their giant, birdlike spaceship that protected Earth from an evil alien named Gallacter. A year later *Space Battleship Yamato* was imported for broadcast in the United States, although American producers changed the name to *Star Blazers*.

As in the *Astro Boy* era, the new shows underwent a considerable amount of editing. They were dubbed into English, and to satisfy the network censors the violence was still being chopped out. Said Patten:

> Early anime fandom had a strongly evangelical fervor. Many fans did not mind watching untranslated anime videos for the visual drama alone. When *Battle of the Planets* and *Star Blazers* spread through syndication around America, there was the thrill of being "in the know" about what the original anime was like. Anime fans would show videos of the unedited Japanese episodes and point out all the scenes of violence that had been censored.[10]

Indeed, American anime fans knew the best parts of the Japanese shows were being cut out of the versions they were seeing on their TV sets in the United States. They also knew that the shows that were being produced in Japan often ventured into topics that were far more thought provoking than what the American producers had chosen to import. For example, a show that hit Japanese airwaves in 1982 was titled *Xabungle*, which was something of a space comedy. In the series, the main character Xabungle (the name is taken from the Japanese word for "bungler") is an inept robot on a quest to find the truth about the death of his father. He

The hit Japanese series *Macross,* known to U.S. television viewers as *Robotech,* played like a soap opera. The show was later turned into a video game (pictured).

engaged in many humorous battles, often set against a background that more closely resembled the American Wild West. But while audiences laughed, they also had to ponder some significant themes. In Xabungle's world, a class struggle existed between the privileged Innocents, who lived in luxury inside a glass dome, and the lowly Civilians, who had to perform manual labor outside the dome in the hostile environment of the planet Zola.

Another show that debuted on Japanese TV in 1982 was *Macross,* which told the story of a team of young heroes who repair and pilot a giant starship that had crashed into Earth. The show was based on the premise that the aliens who constructed the starship, the Zentraedi, were a warlike people descended from the same ancestors as humans. While audiences pondered the question of whether humans were headed down the same path as the Zentraedi, there was a lot more in *Macross* to keep viewers occupied. The show featured a heavy dose of romance among its characters. It was also a musical. Each week one of the characters performed a song; later, albums of *Macross* hits were sold to the show's fans.

In 1985 American TV producer Carl Macek imported *Macross* for American viewers. In the United States the show was aired under the title *Robotech*. Macek actually combined *Macross* with two other anime shows and had the final version dubbed into English. Nevertheless, he left in the romance, the thought-provoking themes, and the violence. (By now, network TV censors were not quite as strict as they had been in the 1960s and 1970s.) Said Macek,

> *Macross* has elements that are completely unknown to American TV cartoons, but are common to comic-book readers and moviegoers. It has a realistic war story in which some of the major good guys get killed. There are robots and space battles, but the plot is really a soap opera that emphasizes the continuing relationships between people. Earth's civilization gets wiped out about three-quarters through the series, not just to show off spectacular violence but as an important, serious plot development. . . . *Macross* is an animated cartoon that fans who think they've outgrown TV cartoons have been waiting for without knowing it. [11]

Postapocalyptic World

Robotech would be followed by other imported shows that greatly expanded the anime available to American audiences. Indeed, throughout the 1980s anime developed a cult-like following. Entrepreneurs established magazines to keep fans abreast of the exploits of top anime characters as well as news about the shows and studios. Bookstores stocked manga titles. Organizations of fans started forming, particularly on college campuses. The biggest group organized during the 1980s was the Earth Defense Command Animation Society, which held its first national con-

vention in Dallas, Texas, in 1990. An even bigger convention, Anime Expo—known among fans as the "AX"—made its debut in 1992 and is held annually in Los Angeles. In 2006 some forty-one thousand anime fans attended the four-day event, which was an impressive 25 percent increase over the 2005 attendance.

With an established audience in America for anime, the movie industry found room for Japanese animation in American theaters. A major anime film featured in American multiplexes was the futuristic supernatural thriller *Akira*, which was released in 1990. The film told of a postapocalyptic world that is starting to rebuild itself when an old nemesis returns, a biological weapon named Akira. The film is set in 2019, a time when biker gangs rule the city streets and the government is manipulated by evil corporate interests—themes well beyond the simple stories found in *Astro Boy* and *Kimba* or even the save-the-planet plots of *Space Battleship Yamato*. What is more, *Akira* was also a technological achievement. The filmmakers were among the first anime producers to use computers to create some of the animation in the film, a process that had been used in the same year in the United States by the Disney

The futuristic supernatural thriller *Akira* is set in a postapocalyptic world ruled by biker gangs and evil corporations.

studio, which had employed computers in the production of *The Little Mermaid*. "*Akira* is almost single-handedly responsible for the early 1990s boom in anime in the English language," said Clements and McCarthy. "*Akira* was a visual tour-de-force, including experiments in digital . . . animation that were to stun audiences worldwide, enjoying greater success abroad than in its country of origin."[12]

SPIRITED AWAY DIRECTOR HAYAO MIYAZAKI

The first anime director to win an Academy Award, Hayao Miyazaki, is one of Japan's most influential and successful filmmakers. Born in 1941, Miyazaki turned to art at an early age. His family owned a factory that manufactured parts for airplanes. As a child, he would accompany his father to the plant, where he enjoyed drawing the planes. His interest in art led to a career in anime.

After graduating from college in 1963, Miyazaki found a job in an animation studio. In 1985 he founded his own production company, Studio Ghibli, which has become one of Japan's most successful anime studios.

Many of Ghibli's films feature young girls as the central characters. Faced with overwhelming challenges as well as personal crises, Miyazaki's heroines always find a means to prevail. Before releasing *Spirited Away*, Miyazaki directed *Princess Mononoke*, a story set in medieval Japan in which guardian spirits must protect a forest from humans, as well as *Kiki's Delivery Service*, a story about a young witch in training who regains her magical powers when she becomes independent and self-reliant.

"He's a wonderfully creative storyteller who has somehow found a way to tell the stories that he wants and that puts him in an incredibly small bracket of writer-directors worldwide," said American anime authority Jonathan Clements.

Quoted in Tim Morrison, "Hayao Miyazaki," *Time*, November 5, 2006. www.time.com/time/magazine/article/0,9171,1554962,00.html.

American film critic Janet Maslin praised the film's director, Katsuhiro Otomo, for the quality of the animation. She wrote,

> Mr. Otomo and his army of highly skilled animators are at their best for conjuring up wildly turbulent special effects, which are rendered with great energy and ingenuity. *Akira* presents dozens of variations on the image of billowing smoke, in every imaginable range of colors. And when its characters hurtle through space, they do it with breathtaking energy. Among the film's typically strange and arresting sequences are one that shows tiny nursery toys transformed into huge, terrifying monsters, and another in which huge, frightening gobs of protoplasm spring out of the body of a frightened victim. [13]

Live-Action Adaptations

There is no question that anime had grown into a commercially successful venture in the United States and that films like *Akira* proved that anime could also compete on an artistic level against American-produced animation. Perhaps the crowning achievement in anime occurred at the 2003 Academy Awards, when the film *Spirited Away* was awarded the Oscar for best animated feature, beating out such films as *Lilo & Stitch* and box office titan *Ice Age*. Directed by Hayao Miyazaki, one of Japan's most influential anime filmmakers, *Spirited Away* is the first anime film to win Hollywood's most prestigious award. The film tells the story of a young girl named Chihiro who enters a world of spirits where she must save a boy who has changed into a dragon. She must also save her parents, who have been turned into pigs.

American film critic Roger Ebert praised the production values of *Spirited Away*—giving weight to the argument that anime had finally caught up to American animation in terms of quality. He also praised the filmmakers for maintaining an atmosphere of Japanese culture in the film—largely missing since the *Astro*

The animated film *Spirited Away* won an Academy Award in 2003. Hayao Miyazaki (pictured) was the creative genius behind the film.

Boy days. Most of the film's action takes place in a Japanese bathhouse, an institution for bathing and relaxation that is common in the Asian country but unknown in America. Also, the filmmakers drop in many other references to Japanese culture. For example, Chihiro's parents turn into pigs while eating a meal—with chopsticks. Said Ebert, "It's enchanting and delightful in its own way, and has a good heart. It is the best animated film of recent years."[14]

There is no question that anime will continue to be a part of the entertainment culture in America for years to come. In fact, Hollywood executives have indicated a willingness to adapt anime into other forms of entertainment. Director James Cameron is heading a project to adapt the manga series *Battle Angel Alita* into a live-action film for release in 2009. The film will tell the story of a part-human and part-robot woman named Alita who seeks the truth about her past. Cameron intends to film the story in a three-dimensional format, using some of the most advanced computer-generated imaging techniques that are available to filmmakers today.

Also headed for the screen is a live-action adaptation of the very popular manga and anime series, *Neon Genesis Evangelion*, which is also known as *EVA*. The film will tell the story of three young heroes who have control over an army of robots, which they use to defend Earth from an invading army of monstrous beings known as Angels. Said Chris Oarr, a spokesman for ADV Films, the production company making *EVA*, "It's inevitable that there will be great science fiction movies made from anime, and it will be Hollywood that makes them because Hollywood is best at realizing the epic scale of a movie like *EVA*." [15]

What Makes
Anime Different?

Anybody who has seen anime on the screen or read a manga novel knows there is a quality to the artwork that sets it aside from animation or graphic novels produced in the United States. All anyone has to do is look into the characters' eyes to see the difference.

In virtually all anime the eyes are drawn big and round. That was an innovation introduced by Tezuka. Working under tight budgets, Tezuka knew he had to tell his stories using as few animation cels as possible. Rather than run through a lot of dialogue to help the plot unfold, Tezuka found he could move the stories along through the emotions exhibited in the faces of the characters. And he found the easiest way to relate emotions was through the eyes. So Tezuka made the eyes big and round so that he could easily alter them to show fear, happiness, anger, and other emotions. Today, even though the budgets for anime have grown, anime artists continue to employ Tezuka's technique. It is simply one of the traits of anime that makes it anime.

There are numerous other details, some subtle but others quite apparent, that set anime and manga apart from animation and comic art produced in the United States and elsewhere. Over the years Japanese artists have refined their techniques, and as a result, the artwork their pens and brushes produce is vivid, colorful, and electric—nothing, by far, like the modest drawings that were used to give life to *Astro Boy*. But even after decades of refining the artistic qualities of the genre, there is no question that the look of Japanese animation stands out from the work produced by artists in other countries.

Cuteness Counts

One of the reasons anime and manga stand apart from movie and comic art produced in the United States is an attention to detail common in Japanese culture but often sacrificed in American animation. Christopher Hart, an American cartoonist and art teacher, says that anime and manga artists often strive to reproduce the

Large, round eyes are one of the most recognizable features of anime characters.

tiniest elements in their characters or in the backgrounds of the scenes. Hart says,

> What makes anime such an instantly recognizable style? Certainly, the character design is unique, focusing on large eyes and subtle features. But beneath it all is a philosophy that captures the essence of the anime spirit.

> Western-style animation expresses itself primarily through movement. The more a character moves, the "better" the animation is thought to be. So, it's not surprising that animation producers in the West typically redesign comic book characters for television, simplifying them to allow for greater movement. Although anime characters are also licensed from comic books, emphasis is placed on retaining the integrity of the original comic. The detail and subtlety in the drawings are not sacrificed to allow for greater movement. As a result, anime has the appearance of a real comic book come to life![16]

Anime artists use vivid colors and intricate detail to electrify background scenes.

Although Tezuka had financial reasons for drawing wide saucer eyes, he also found the look was appealing to audiences. Indeed, one of the reasons that Japanese anime artists have decided to retain Tezuka's style for drawing eyes is that it makes the characters look cute. Japanese culture places a lot of emphasis on cuteness. In Japan the interiors of airliners are decorated with paintings of Pokémon characters—the little pocket monsters can even be found on the headrests of the seats and on the plastic drinking cups distributed by the flight attendants. Earth-moving equipment is painted to resemble zoo animals—zebra-striped bulldozers are common sights on construction jobs. Meanwhile, each Japanese police station has its own cartoon mascot, and the tiny kiosks that shelter Japanese traffic cops from the weather are designed to resemble gingerbread houses. In Japanese baseball a player who hits a home run is traditionally rewarded with a stuffed animal when he crosses the plate. One of the most popular tattoos in Japan is an image of Badtz-Maru, a cartoon penguin. (Even cute American characters have found a home in Japan; Cookie Monster's furry blue face can be found adorning cell phones in Japan).

And so, in a culture that values cuteness it should come as no surprise that in anime and manga, artists take steps to make sure their characters retain an element of cuteness—even in stories that are otherwise punctuated by violence and end-of-the-world themes. Said Poitras, "Large eyes are favored in a culture like Japan's that puts such a high value on 'cuteness.' Large eyes are often used to express innocence, and younger characters will often have eyes larger than those of adults."[17]

Apart from the eyes, the other most obvious feature found in the face of a Japanese anime character is that he or she rarely appears to be Japanese. Most characters found in anime or manga appear to be of Western ethnicity. This style dates back to the earliest years of anime in the 1950s. At the time, anime was in competition with live-action films for ticket sales among Japanese audiences. Because the Japanese live-action movie companies operated under extremely tight budgets, the films had to be produced in Japan using Japanese actors. As such, the plots were limited to stories

THE POKÉMON CRAZE

Millions of young American children have been caught up in the Pokémon craze that landed in the United States in 1998. Conceived first as a video game—players caught a series of characters known as "pocket monsters"—the characters eventually evolved into comic books as well as a feature film and a series broadcast on American TV. In 1999 the first Pokémon comic book published in the United States sold more than a million copies.

Since then, Pokémon has become a worldwide phenomenon. The *Pokémon* TV series is now seen in nearly seventy countries worldwide. In all, the Pokémon video games, trading cards, comic books, films, and TV series have earned Nintendo, the Japanese video game manufacturer that owns the series, more than $4 billion in the decade since the pocket monsters made their first appearance.

One retailer in Toronto, Canada, told a news reporter that she cannot keep Pokémon trading cards in stock. "It's crazy—we order 200 cases at a time, but they send us only two," said Julie Bernadelli of the Hairy Tarantula card and game shop in Toronto. "If we could get all the Pokémon we could sell, we all could retire."

The Pokémon characters were conceived by Satoshi Tajiri, a reclusive Japanese video game designer who drew on memories of his childhood when he designed the characters, basing them on insects he collected as a boy as well as the monsters he saw featured in old horror movies.

Quoted in James Deacon and Susan McClelland, "The Craze That Ate Your Kids," *Maclean's*, November 8, 1999, p. 74.

about domestic life in Japan. Anime artists found that by using Western faces in their stories, they could give them an international flavor and center the stories in any country they desired. That helped the anime producers lure Japanese audiences, who were eager to see movies, even animated movies, about America and Europe. And so today, even though an anime character may have a Japanese name, eat with chopsticks, and wear a kimono, her face will make it appear that she is as American as Lois Lane.

Conveying Action and Drama

The hair colors found on the heads of anime and manga characters also add to the Western looks of the characters. Most Japanese people have black hair or very dark brown hair. In anime, hair colors vary widely, from dark tones to blond to red to some wild incandescent shades. In manga, hair still comes mostly in three colors: black, white, or gray. That is because manga is printed mostly in black and white.

Outside Japan comic artists frequently use hair color to identify characters so that a reader can easily recognize a character in the scene. (Would eternal teenager Archie be so easily recognized without his bright orange hair? Or his girlfriend Betty without her blond ponytail?) Since manga artists are generally restricted to working in black and white, they compensate by drawing wild and distinct hairstyles. Since the artists cannot identify their characters by hair color, they draw hairstyles in wild and bouncy styles so that the reader can easily pick out the characters in the manga frame. Once manga was adapted into anime the hairstyles were adapted as well, although now the artists could make them even wilder by adding color. Today, some manga is published in color, but even in color manga characters are drawn with outlandish hairstyles—it is simply a holdover from the days when the manga artists were forced to work strictly in black and white.

To an anime artist, hair can be used for purposes other than to identify a character or to help illustrate the character's personality. Anime artists have found they can use hair to convey emotions, action, and drama. Said Poitras,

> The movement of a character's hair is quite noticeable in anime. Hair flows in the breeze, moves when the character shifts suddenly, or comes to a halt. It gets wild during

battle, and settles during a moment of stillness. A character may be pensive, with eyes cast downward, and a small lock of hair will come loose from behind an ear at a visually interesting moment. "Hair action" thus adds to the atmosphere of scenes and enhances the behaviors and feelings of the characters. It requires more complex cels and makes the anime more expensive, but the effect is a powerful one and adds much to one's viewing pleasure.[18]

The movement of a character's hair helps convey emotions such as astonishment, which can be seen in the face of the central character from *Spirited Away.*

In anime, movement is also conveyed in how the characters are portrayed as they walk, run, and make other motions. For example, anime characters bend low when they run, which helps create the illusion of speed. But when they walk, anime characters walk tall and with authority. Anime artists often find that they can best animate conversations if their characters are walking while they are talking. Said Hart, "Whereas the typical anime

run is portrayed as an all-out panic, the anime walk is restrained. The body is upright and stiff. The walk is used mainly during conversations between characters in which they coolly discuss the strategic problems of waging war against their enemies."[19]

Meanwhile, in the background the soundtrack of the scene often includes the noise made by the characters' feet hitting the ground. "Sometimes, I think the best thing about the typical anime walk is the sound effect," said Hart. "The lonely sound of footsteps echoing through an empty corridor is charged with atmosphere."[20]

Backgrounds of anime scenes have, in fact, become much more sophisticated in recent years. In the *Astro Boy* days a background was essentially a painted picture—the scene never changed although the characters moved their feet. With larger budgets with which to work, Japanese animators have improved the backgrounds in the scenes. Anime artists have found they can give the stories more depth if they provide a sense of movement in the backgrounds. Said Poitras,

> Overall, Japanese backgrounds are more likely to be in motion and to change and turn. Obviously, this costs more money, which is why a lot of American studios avoid the effect. Not all anime uses a dynamic background, but much of it does, along with other cinematic effects like pan shots, angles, distance shots, scenes where the focus between the foreground and background changes, and so on.[21]

Reading Manga

In Japan comic art is not only drawn differently than in America but it is also read differently. While there is no question that in America comic books appeal mostly to a youthful audience, Japanese manga is read by fans who range from young children to adults; as such, it is written and drawn on different levels. Each genre has its own category. For example, boys between the ages of six and eighteen are likely to read titles known as *shonen*, which

MANGA ON SUNDAYS

Newspapers in America have taken the first tentative steps toward publishing manga in their Sunday comics sections. Starting in 2006 two manga series, *Van Von Hunter* and *Peach Fuzz,* started appearing in a handful of American newspapers.

The two series are written and drawn by American artists, but they are distributed by Tokyopop, the Japanese manga publisher. Both series are aimed at young audiences. *Van Von Hunter* is a humorous series about a warrior and his sidekick who battle evil, although they are often rather confused about who is and is not a villain. *Peach Fuzz* tells the story of nine-year-old Amanda and her pet ferret, Peach.

Newspaper executives said they decided to start publishing manga to lure younger readers. According to industry statistics, the average age of the American newspaper reader is fifty-three. Said John Glynn, vice president of Universal Press Syndicate, which distributes the manga series, "I know how popular manga and anime are among a young demographic. Go to any bookstore and there are kids swarming around the manga shelves. And by kids I mean everyone from high school into their 30s. But this trend clearly hasn't made itself felt in newspaper comic sections."

Quoted in Yuri Kageyama, "Papers and Japanese-Style Comics to Attract Young Set," Associated Press, *Pittsburgh Post-Gazette,* November. 8, 2004, p. E-2.

is the Japanese word for "boy." Shonen titles predominantly feature action and adventure stories. Shonen is by far the most popular manga in Japan with several magazines devoted to the genre. The largest is *Jump,* a weekly with a circulation of some 6 million readers. In comparison, America's largest magazine, *Time,* which features news and commentary on current events, has a circulation of about 4 million readers a week.

Young girls read *shojo*, which is the Japanese word for "girl." Readers of shojo are usually under twelve. Shojo stories focus on strong relationships among the female protagonists. One of the most popular shojo series is *Peach Girl*, which has been adapted into an anime series and even a live-action stage play. *Peach Girl* tells the story of Momo, a blond-haired teenage girl who must endure the taunts, rumor-passing, and backstabbing of the other girls in her high school.

Girls over twelve read *shonen ai*, which means "boy love" stories. These stories also focus on strong relationships among the female protagonists, but shonen ai also introduces romance into the stories. One of the most popular shonen ai series is *Gravitation*, which has also been adapted into an anime series. *Gravitation* tells the story of the young musicians of a struggling rock band.

A Japanese youth reads a manga adventure tale in a Tokyo café.

Men over the age of eighteen read *seinen*, or "adult," manga. In seinen manga, the violence is quite graphic while the skirts worn by the female characters tend to be quite short. There are dozens of successful seinen titles and several publications with large circulations that specialize in seinen manga. One of the most popular seinen series in Japan today is *Blade of the Immortal*, which tells the story of an immortal samurai swordsman on a quest to kill one thousand evil men.

THE OTAKU

In America devoted fans of the old television series *Star Trek* are known as "Trekkies." These are fans who watch reruns of the show religiously, read the books based on the show, and attend conventions where they buy and swap *Star Trek* merchandise and seek autographs from some of the show's former performers. Japan has its version of the Trekkies. They are known as the "otaku," a name given to fans obsessed with manga and anime.

In fact, a neighborhood in Tokyo is known as "Otaku Town." The neighborhood features dozens of stores that sell manga and anime. Many manga cafés are also located in Otaku Town; they cater to the mostly college-aged clientele that gathers to talk about manga and anime and trade books and merchandise. In the cafés the waitresses dress as manga characters. Otaku also dress up as manga characters and attend parties known as "cosplays"—short for "costume plays."

Otaku can also be found in America. Susan Napier, a professor at the University of Texas at Austin, said otaku clubs and cosplay parties started forming on campus in the early 1990s. At first most of the members were Asian American students, but in recent years the membership has become more diverse. "African American, Hispanics, and even Muslim students are drawn to it," she said. "Otaku are also more gender-equal than in the past."

Quoted in "Obsessed with Anime," *Chronicle of Higher Education*, July 28, 2006, p. A-33.

Different styles of manga, some of which appear here, appeal to different readers.

Women over the age of eighteen read *josei*, which is a Japanese word for "adult women." Josei manga usually centers on contemporary stories of women dealing with crises in their relationships and professional lives. One of the most successful josei series in Japan is *Paradise Kiss*, which tells the story of a young model named Yukari who must deal with the cutthroat world of high fashion. *Paradise Kiss* is also a very well-watched anime series on Japanese TV.

Right to Left

Josei, seinen, and the other categories of manga are available on the shelves of bookstores in America. American readers will find them much fatter than the typical comic books and even heftier than English-language graphic novels. Manga titles sometimes span several hundred pages.

Also, comic book readers are used to square or rectangular frames that enable the eye to easily follow the action across and then down the page. In manga the artists regard the shape of the frame as a component of the creative process. In manga the frames are irregularly shaped, often in a jagged design, and they fit together on the page like a jigsaw puzzle.

In addition to dealing with a jigsaw-style page of pictures, new fans of manga should be aware that when they first pick a manga title off the shelf they may be in for something of a surprise: The book is likely to open from the wrong side.

That is because the Japanese read from right to left. Although the books are translated into English, most publishers will keep the right-to-left orientation. At first American readers may find it difficult to follow the stories, but most manga fans eventually train their eyes to follow the action.

Some manga titles are published in a left-to-right format. This involves the practice known as "flipping," in which the images are printed backward. Most of the time the transition will be seamless, but occasionally humorous little details emerge. For example, a reader may notice a car's steering wheel on the wrong side of the vehicle. A thug whom the artist has named "Lefty" may seem to always use his right hand. Manga fans learn to tolerate flipping.

The Princess Diaries series of books has spawned movies (a scene from one of the movies is shown here) and a manga version of the books is next.

Actually, manga flipping may one day cease to be a problem for American readers because publishers in the United States have started making plans to publish their own manga. Starting in 2007 HarperCollins, one of America's largest book publishers, intends to collaborate with a Japanese manga publisher, Tokyopop, to produce a new series of titles featuring the work of American authors. The first author whose work is expected to be adapted into a manga format is Meg Cabot, the author of The Princess Diaries and Avalon High series of books for young readers. Other American publishers, including Random House and Simon & Schuster, have also established their own manga divisions or struck deals with Japanese publishers to distribute manga in America.

Jane Collins, the chief executive officer of HarperCollins, said she has long wanted to start a manga division at the New York–based publisher but realized that her company lacks the expertise to produce its own manga titles. She pointed out that there are few manga artists working in the United States today, and that is why the participation of a Tokyo-based publisher is necessary to adapt U.S. titles into the format. Meanwhile, she said, HarperCollins owns the rights to a wealth of literature for young readers that have until now been unavailable to the Japanese manga publishers. "We've got great young adult and children's authors and we're going to take a careful long look at that list,"[22] Collins said.

And so it appears that manga is on the verge of tremendous growth in the United States. It is possible that dozens or even hundreds of the most familiar titles on American bookshelves may soon be told in the unique style of the Japanese manga artist.

The Role of
Women in Anime

O ne animated Japanese show that made a successful transition to American TV was *Sailor Moon*, which debuted in the early 1990s and until recently aired in syndication in the United States. The story started out as a manga series in Japan and was then animated into a TV series with more than two hundred episodes as well as three feature films. (It has even been produced as a live-action TV show in Japan as well as a Broadway-style musical on stage.) The series tells the story of a teenage girl named Serena who calls on magical powers to transform into the heroine Sailor Moon. She is accompanied by the Sailor Warriors—Sailor Mercury, Sailor Venus, and others—who assist her in battles against the forces of evil.

The series is clearly aimed at a preteen-girl audience. It depicts teenage girls as strong, intelligent, brave, and able to accomplish heroic deeds without relying on their boyfriends or fathers to come to their rescue. But it also treats the characters as much more than super beings; in the series, Serena and the other Sailor Warriors explore their emotions and grow and mature as the stories unfold.

By examining such content, *Sailor Moon* and other anime films and TV shows prove to be years if not decades ahead of American animation, as well as literature, in depicting women as equals to men. After all, when the series debuted in America, girls who watched Sailor Moon outwit the evil Queen Beryl on TV had just recently seen the Disney version of *The Little Mermaid*, in which Prince Eric had to rescue Ariel from the clutches of Ursula, the sea witch. And the generations of girls who read about the adventures of teenage sleuth Nancy Drew inevitably came to the point in each story when Nancy's football-star boyfriend, Ned Nickerson, had to be called on to break down a door or punch the villain in the nose.

But in anime female characters usually take care of business themselves. In the 1997 film *Princess Mononoke*, the two main characters are female: Princess Mononoke, the teenage girl raised by

Sailor Moon tells the story of a teenage girl who fights evil with magic. She and her companions are strong, intelligent, and brave.

NAOKO TAKEUCHI, CREATOR OF *SAILOR MOON*

The creator of *Sailor Moon* never intended to be an artist. Born in 1967, Naoko Takeuchi majored in chemistry in college. After receiving her degree from Kyoritsu Yakka University in Tokyo, Takeuchi found a job as a pharmacist at Keio Hospital in the Japanese city of Ise. She was always interested in art, though, and started drawing as a young girl.

As a college student she produced her first professional manga title, "Love Call," which was published in a major manga magazine in Japan. She also developed a manga series, *Cherry Project*, which told the story of young figure skaters.

While working at the hospital pharmacy, the editor of a manga magazine suggested she develop a series about teenage girls who wear sailor uniforms, which is a standard dress code for junior high and high school girls in Japan. The series Takeuchi created, a story about a girl with magical powers, was originally titled *Codename Sailor V* and made its debut in 1991. After refining the concept, Takeuchi developed the series *Sailor Moon*, about a team of girls, which debuted a year later in manga and anime. Takeuchi later said that she accepted the suggestion of the characters wearing sailor uniforms because she knew junior high and high school can be difficult years for girls, and she felt they needed a hero who would represent them in manga and anime.

wolves who fights to protect the wildlife of the forest, and Lady Eboshi, the ruler of Irontown, where iron miners seek to exploit the abundant resources in the forest. Princess Mononoke and Lady Eboshi are both fearless leaders and relentless warriors. Given the gender of the main characters, it would seem as though *Princess Mononoke*, like *Sailor Moon*, was written mostly for an audience of young girls, but that is not true. Directed by Miyazaki, *Princess Mononoke* became the top-grossing movie of all time in Japan until it was displaced by the blockbuster American film *Titanic*, meaning that audiences of all ages and both genders were enthralled by the adventures of the wolf princess and her adversary, and it did not seem to matter to them that the male characters were of secondary importance to the plot.

Respect for Women

The fact that Princess Mononoke and Sailor Moon emerged from Japanese culture may be even more surprising to American fans, given that the overriding Western notion of Japanese women finds them to be quiet, passive, and submissive to men. In other words, they are all supposed to be like geisha girls, not like the Sailor Warriors.

Princess Mononoke, in the movie of the same name, is a determined warrior and leader who battles to protect the wild animals of the forest.

Strong female characters appear in many anime stories and films.

But that is a myth, according to Price. She said the Japanese Shinto religion respects women and reserves an important place for them in society. There is no question that Japanese animators bring their beliefs to the drawing table. Said Price,

Unlike much of Western folklore and heroics, many of the ancient Japanese tales of gods and demons are composed of female deities and spirits. Japanese history is also dominated by powerful empresses, priestesses, writers and artisans. As a result, anime is chock full of female protagonists and villains. Contrary to the subservient geisha stereotype of Japanese women, Japanese society is quite tolerant of strong women in the family and the workplace, quite possibly because ancient history and Shinto belief are filled with powerful heroines that played prominent roles in the shaping of Japan.[23]

In addition to religious influences, there may also be cultural influences in Japan that encourage the depiction of females as strong, independent characters. British journalist John Gosling, who frequently writes about the anime industry, suggested that Japanese boys are far more devoted to their mothers than their fathers. In the typical Japanese home a father is up before dawn and on the train to work before his children rise for school. Frequently, he will not arrive home until after the children are asleep. In other words, Japanese children rarely see their fathers and are much more influenced by their mothers. Said Gosling,

> To understand why it is that women are so often key characters in anime, I think you have to look at the Japanese home, and specifically the relationship between children and their mothers, particularly male children and their mothers. . . . In a climate where women call their seldom seen husbands "oversize garbage" and "wet leaves" because they stick to everything and are hard to sweep up, is it any wonder that boys fixate on their mothers and make them super heroines?[24]

It is not surprising that *Sailor Moon* and similar shows were a hit in Japan before they arrived in America. Girls and women are dedicated readers of manga in Japan—and not just the shojo, shonen ai, and josei categories written specifically for female readers. Indeed, it is estimated that some 30 percent of all manga published in Japan is aimed directly at women, but girls and women also read a lot of manga written for both sexes or written specifically for boys and men. With so many dedicated female readers, it is obvious that the manga publishers would risk losing fans if female characters were constantly portrayed as helpless victims who need strong male heroes to rescue them—as they frequently are in American movies and comic books.

Changing Attitude

Actually, that attitude is starting to change—no doubt thanks to the example set by Japanese manga publishers and anime producers. In 2007, U.S.-based DC Comics announced it would publish a new series of graphic novels aimed specifically at teenage girls. The novels are not intended to feature science fiction, fantasy, or superhero story lines—a staple of DC's business—but instead center on stories of girls being girls, dealing with the pressures and responsibilities of growing up in America. One of the first graphic novels in the series, *The P.L.A.I.N. Janes,* will feature four protagonists, all named Jane, who start a club called People Loving Art in the Neighborhoods. Their club will take on a variety of causes, from protesting construction of a new mall to campaigning to save unwanted pets. Novels in the series will be written by women. Said Johanna Draper Carlson, the editor of the comic book criticism Web site comicsworthreading.com, "When you had mostly

ANIME'S DARK SIDE

There is a dark side to anime and manga. It can be particularly violent and pornographic. This form of manga and anime is known as *hentai,* a Japanese word that means "abnormality." Women, who are otherwise given important roles as central characters in most anime and manga, can also be depicted as the victims of brutal abuse. Some manga series have been so objectionable that the publishers have been forced to pull them from the shelves due to complaints raised by women's groups.

Said Andrew Pollack, the Tokyo correspondent for the *New York Times,* "One reason Japanese comics and animation get away with sex and violence is that they are not just for children. Some of the same blue-suited businessmen who have made Japan into an economic superpower commute to work on the subways reading comic books, some as thick as telephone books and many sexually explicit."

Japan has a relatively low crime rate. Also, laws in Japan prevent sexually explicit and violent manga and anime from being sold to minors. Nevertheless, the police occasionally report that violent crimes have been committed by individuals who confess that they were influenced by their favorite manga and anime titles.

Andrew Pollack, "Japan, a Superpower Among Superheroes," *New York Times,* September 17, 1995, p. 32.

boys and men making comics, you had comics made mainly for boys and men. Then you end up with teen-girl superheroes who are drawn like Victoria's Secret models."[25]

Clearly, the American publishers are waking up to what pre-teen and teenage girls want to read. For years girls who browsed through American comic book stores saw titles devoted to such male-dominated series as *Batman*, *Superman*, and *Spider-Man*. Is it any wonder that they soon lost interest in comic literature? Matt Thorn, a Harvard University scholar of Japanese culture who has studied manga, said, "Girls would read *Archie* comics until they turned 10 or 11, then read youth novels or teen novels."[26]

When manga started arriving on bookstore shelves, girls were immediately attracted to the stories. Jenna Leary, an eighteen-year-old college student from California, was drawn to manga as an eleven-year-old, when she became a fan of *Sailor Moon* and discovered that her favorite cartoon character on TV could also be found on the pages of graphic novels. Since then she has collected nearly two hundred manga titles. When she has the money, she spends as much as fifty or sixty dollars a week on manga. As a college student, her taste has evolved from shojo and shonen ai to the action and adventure stories more typically read by men. She is, for example, a big fan of the anime film *Akira*. "My friends decided I needed to go to a manga anonymous meeting because I have an addiction problem,"[27] said Leary.

Another young fan, seventeen-year-old Christa Newman of Kingston, Massachusetts, said she owns seventy-five manga titles. She also makes her own costumes that she wears to cosplays, the parties attended by manga fanatics. Newman has attended cosplays dressed as Michiru, a character in *Sailor Moon*, and Yukari, the main character in *Paradise Kiss*. "I just love the art form and how the characters are so much more developed than regular cartoons and comic books," said Newman. "I love the characters. I also love sewing. So it kind of went hand in hand."[28]

Growing and Maturing

Sailor Moon and *Paradise Kiss* are both drawn by female manga artists. While American comic book publishers are just starting to recruit women writers and artists, Japanese manga and anime have long been written and drawn by women who are among the country's most successful artists. Said Poitras, "Women play a major role in the industry as writers, artists, and animators—far beyond what is seen in other countries—and this shows in the kinds of programs being made."[29] *Paradise Kiss* is written and drawn by Ai Yazawa, who has produced more than a dozen successful manga series, all aimed at female audiences. *Sailor Moon* was conceived by manga artist Naoko Takeuchi, who gave up her job as a pharmacist to concentrate on a career in manga. In *Sailor Moon*, Serena is an ordinary schoolgirl—sailor uniforms are mandatory apparel at her school—whose long-dormant powers are awakened when she learns that Earth is under attack by sinister forces. As the series progressed, Serena grew as a person. She started out as a clumsy fourteen-year-old who is something of a crybaby. As she slowly discovered her powers, she grew braver and more aware of the needs of others. As her story unfolded, Serena grew older and more mature and found romance.

In the meantime, Takeuchi gave her super-powered heroine some very real human emotions. That is a familiar trend among most female manga and anime artists working in Japan. Among the most successful manga artists in Japan are four women who compose their manga under the pseudonym Clamp. (The letters in the name make up an abbreviation of Japanese words that translates roughly into "pile of potatoes.") Clamp started out as a circle of eleven female art students who got together to compose *doujinshi*, which is amateur manga. Typically, doujinshi takes the adventures of popular manga characters beyond where their published stories leave off.

Some doujinshi artists graduate into the professional ranks, and that is what happened to Clamp in 1989. After some initial successes in publishing professional manga, seven of the artists dropped out to forge their own careers. The four remaining Clamp members have evolved into a very successful team; they are responsible for the production of more than twenty well-read manga series, many of which have been adapted into anime. Many of their anime titles have been dubbed into English and imported

into the United States, where they are available in DVD format. "Clamp have been an integral part of the manga explosion that's occurred in the U.S. over the past several years," said Dallas Middaugh, an executive with the American publisher Random House, which has recently established a manga division. "Their fluid, dramatic artwork and storytelling struck a strong chord with male and female manga readers."[30]

One of Clamp's most popular series is *Tsubasa*, which has sold more than a million copies in the United States. The series has also been adapted into anime, which has been made available for sale in the United States on DVD. *Tsubasa* tells the story of four young adventurers who travel into other dimensions to retrieve the feathers from the wings of a princess spirit, who will die without them. Like Serena of *Sailor Moon*, the princess spirit of *Tsubasa*, a character named Sakura, is also presented as a very human girl who grows and matures as the series progresses. In

Artist Naoko Takeuchi gave the super-powered heroine of *Sailor Moon* (center, top) real emotions and allowed her to grow and mature in the role.

fact, Clamp adapted Sakura into *Tsubasa* from another anime and manga series titled *Card Captor Sakura*, which was aimed at younger children. In *Card Captor Sakura*, ten-year-old Sakura discovers her powers when she inadvertently releases evil spirits from a deck of cards. In the series she is charged with the task of retrieving the spirits and returning them to the deck. Therefore, Clamp has taken a precocious little girl and transformed her into a troubled teenager—an evolution with which most teenage girls, whether they are Japanese or American, can easily relate. Said Ageha Ohkawa, one of the members of Clamp, "It's common in girls' manga for a character to transform, as Sailor Moon does, and we wanted to incorporate that into Sakura."[31]

Young women in Japan have many choices when it comes to manga that feature vibrant female characters.

Confronting Women's Issues

One manga character who undergoes a dramatic transformation is Ranma Saotome, the featured character in the series *Ranma ½*. The series, which confronts women's issues head-on, was created by Rumiko Takahashi, one of the most successful manga artists in Japan. Fans of her work have bought more than 100 million copies of her manga titles—making her one of the wealthiest women in Japan. Many of Takahashi's titles have also been adapted into anime. Takahashi's titles have run the full spectrum of manga and anime genres: science fiction stories, martial arts dramas, mythological adventures, romantic tales, and coming-of-age stories.

Ranma ½ is Takahaski's most popular, and probably her quirkiest, series. In *Ranma ½*, which is a manga series, anime series, and feature film, the main character falls into a magical spring; when he emerges Ranma finds that he changes into a girl whenever he is splashed with cold water. (He changes back after he is splashed with hot water; his father, who fell into the same spring, changes into a panda bear.) As a girl, Ranma encounters discrimination as well as unwanted sexual advances from teenage boys. But when he fights as a girl, he employs techniques of cunning, intelligence, agility, and speed he does not think of using when he fights as a boy.

But even that causes him trouble. When Ranma, as a girl, wins a martial arts competition, he faces bitterness from his male friends because they still do not believe his fighting ability measures up to what he could accomplish as a male fighter. Said Susan J. Napier, "Although he wins in the end, his friends have little confidence in him because they are aware that even his martial arts expertise may not make up for his female limitations. Ranma's girlishness thus adds an extra tension to an already intense action sequence." [32]

Ranma ½ has never received broadcast or theatrical exposure in the United States, but episodes are available on video and DVD in America as well as other countries. *Ranma ½* is intended as a comedy, but there is no question that the issues confronted in the series are taken very seriously by contemporary girls and women.

5

The Messages of Anime

I n the anime film *Grave of the Fireflies,* two orphans wander through a war-devastated Japan after their village is destroyed by enemy bombs. Things get even bleaker for Seita and Setsuko. After finding life with an evil aunt unbearable, Seita and Setsuko make their way to an air raid shelter where they beg for food or steal what they can. Finally, Seita and Setsuko die from starvation.

As the film shows, there is more to anime and manga than science fiction, sword and sorcery tales, and adventure stories. Sometimes anime comes with a clear and often disturbing social message. Certainly Japan's unique place in history as the only country ever to have been attacked by atomic weapons has a lot to do with why a lot of anime and manga deliver intense anti-war messages.

But anime and manga also tackle other contemporary issues. Environmental themes are common in anime and manga. Many stories speak up for oppressed minorities. Anime and manga artists often dwell on philosophical issues, such as whether human culture and traditions can adapt to technology. Said Price, "Anime often disguises contemporary struggles and themes in its entertaining medium. The fact that so many anime shows and movies take place in futuristic or ancient worlds of social upheaval and political unrest says a lot about the current mind of Japanese animators."[33]

Japanese Version of History

Anime has had a purpose other than entertainment since the days when the Japanese Imperial Navy drafted Momotaro to help boost the morale of audiences during World War II. The war was, of course, brought to an abrupt conclusion when the United States dropped atomic bombs on the Japanese cities of Hiroshima and Nagasaki. In fact, the Allies had been bombing Japan for months before atomic weapons were unleashed on the island. In one campaign American bombers dropped napalm canisters on several Japanese cities. Napalm is a chemical that erupts into flash fires. It was deployed in containers that resembled tin cans, which looked harmless until they struck the ground. Then, they exploded and burned everything near them.

One of the survivors of the napalm attacks was a teenage boy named Nosaka Akiyuki, who was living in the city of Kobe when the sky suddenly started raining napalm canisters. Akiyuki survived the attack, but his father died in the firestorm, and a sister died of starvation soon after the bombing. Akiyuki based his 1967 novel *Grave of the Fireflies* on his experiences in the Kobe firebombing. The book won the Naoki Award, which is Japan's top prize for literature—similar to the Pulitzer Prize in America. Years later the story was produced as an anime feature film by director Isao Takahata of Studio Ghibli.

Grave of the Fireflies is a movie that promotes deep sympathy for the Japanese people, and it certainly struck a chord among Japanese audiences when it was released. In the years since the end of World War II, the Japanese people have regarded themselves as hapless victims who were led into the conflict by a corrupt and warmongering regime that was dominated by military leaders. This version of history has allowed the Japanese people to remain guilt-free while they bury a sad chapter in their nation's history. *Grave of the Fireflies* supports this vision. Indeed, the film opens with the boy, Seita, succumbing to starvation a month after the end of the war. An adult finds his lifeless body and immediately searches his

Nosaka Akiyuki's novel *Grave of the Fireflies,* and the anime movie that followed, are based on his experiences during the firebombing of Kobe, Japan (pictured).

pockets for something of value. All he finds is a can containing the bones and ashes of Seita's sister, Setsuko.

The story is then told in flashbacks that ignore the many historical facts that led up to the Allied bombing of Japan—the country's invasion of China, the Japanese domination of Korea, and the Imperial Navy's attack on Pearl Harbor, among others. However, the villains in the film are not the Americans who dropped the napalm bombs but the cold-hearted leaders of wartime Japan who led their country into war and let the two children die. Said Clements and McCarthy,

This is an eerily quiet, sepia-toned apocalypse, accompanied by powerful subliminal messages. Throughout the entire film, we regularly return to the ghosts of Seita and Setsuko, lit in red, as they gaze accusingly at the countrymen who let them die. . . . Similarly, director Takahata loads on subtle guilt as to what might have been "if only" the slightest chance had been taken to make a difference. . . . A crushingly sad story, beginning by revealing both characters will die, and then daring the viewer to hope they won't. Tragedy in the truest sense of the word: every moment of Takahata's masterpiece is loaded with portents of the suffering to come. [34]

Grave of the Fireflies was released in American theaters in 1994. American audiences, who generally do not share the view that the Japanese people were helpless victims of the war, were nevertheless moved and sympathetic to the plight of the two doomed children. In 2000, when *Grave of the Fireflies* was released in a DVD version, film critic Roger Ebert said,

Because it is animated and from Japan, *Grave of the Fireflies* has been little seen. When anime fans say how good the film is, nobody takes them seriously. Now that it's available on DVD with a choice of subtitles or English dubbing, maybe it will find the attention it deserves. Yes, it's a cartoon, and the kids have eyes like saucers, but it belongs on any list of the greatest war films ever made. [35]

Atomic Attack

Grave of the Fireflies is essentially the story of a human tragedy. It could easily have been told in a live-action film. Although Takahata used animation to give the film a mystical quality—the ghosts of Seita and Setsuko appear throughout, and a scene in which fireflies illuminate the children's faces in a dark cave is also touching—a studio's special effects crew would have had little trouble creating those images for a live-action film.

But portraying an atomic bomb blast is not as easily accomplished in a live-action movie. In fact, a special-effects replication of an atomic blast would likely horrify audiences. On the other hand, animation may be a far more appropriate medium to show the images of an atomic attack. The 1983 anime film *Barefoot Gen* confronted the atomic holocaust head-on. The film tells the story of a boy who survives the atomic blast at Hiroshima that ended World War II. In the story Gen and his mother watch their family members burned alive by the blast, then witness their

Anime offered filmmakers a way to re-create the atomic bomb blasts over Japan. Pictured is the sky over Nagasaki, Japan, after the American nuclear bomb attack.

friends and neighbors slowly die from radiation poisoning. According to Napier, by employing animation to tell the story the filmmakers can use the art of the animator to show what it was like during an atomic blast. She suggested that by witnessing a live-action reenactment of the Hiroshima blast audience members would become so shocked by the visual spectacle of the explosion that they could miss the point of the story. By watching the story told through the medium of anime, she said, audience members can bear witness to the devastation with the full knowledge that they are, after all, watching nothing more than a cartoon. She said,

> It is precisely the graphics of manga and anime that can help to "convey the unconveyable" of the bomb's horror. The stunning visuals employed in the film to represent the bombing and its aftermath are hideous, painful to look at, and unforgettable. . . . Scenes that even with the contemporary special effects and contemporary values would be difficult to present and watch in live-action film become, in the nonrealistic space of animation, enduring evocations of a genuine hell on earth. [36]

Unlike *Grave of the Fireflies*, which was based on a highly esteemed novel, *Barefoot Gen* was adapted from a story that was originally published as manga. The manga artist, Keiji Nakazawa, is a survivor of Hiroshima and his story is autobiographical.

In 1966, twenty-one years after the atomic bomb dropped on Hiroshima, Nakazawa was living in Tokyo and working as a manga artist. That year, his mother died. She was his only close relative—his other family members perished in the atomic blast. Nakazawa believes she had been afflicted with radiation poisoning as a result of the blast, and that her bones withered away over the years. At that point Nakazawa said he realized how much Japanese culture had discouraged discussion of Hiroshima and Nagasaki—in any medium. To Nakazawa it seemed as though the Japanese people learned to deal with the horrific destruction of two large cities and the deaths of more than

200,000 people simply by keeping silent about the event and pretending that it never happened. He said,

> Since coming to Tokyo, I hadn't said a word about being an A-bomb survivor to anyone. People in Tokyo looked at you very strangely if you talked about it, so I learned to keep quiet. There was still an irrational fear among many Japanese that you could "catch" radiation sickness from A-bomb victims. There were plenty of people like that, even in a big city like Tokyo. [37]

Educating a Generation

And so Nakazawa resolved to use the medium of manga to tell the story of the atomic bomb victims. He soon produced a series, *Struck by Black Rain,* which related the story of Hiroshima survivors turning to crime to survive in postwar Japan. "*Black Rain* was published in serial form in *Manga Punch,* an adult manga magazine by a small publisher," said Nakazawa. "The big publishers turned it down. They said it was too radical for them, too political." [38]

Undaunted by the reaction of the big publishers, Nakazawa continued to produce manga about his experiences in Hiroshima following the atomic blast. Eventually, the manga magazine *Monthly Shonen Jump* decided to publish a series of biographies of manga artists, told in manga form. Nakazawa was invited to submit his own story. He responded by producing an early version of *Barefoot Gen,* which he titled *I Saw It.* The editor of the magazine, Tadasu Nagano, read the story and was awestruck by Nakazawa's experiences in Hiroshima.

> When Nagano read it, he told me, "You should do a longer series based on this. You can make it as many pages as you want and we can run it for as long as you want." I could hardly believe it. That was the first time an editor had ever said anything like that to me. I was incredibly grateful, and felt I should do the best job I could. That was how *Barefoot Gen* came about. [39]

The series ran for nearly two years, until *Monthly Shonen Jump* went out of business. By now *Barefoot Gen* had earned a following in Japan, and Nakazawa had no trouble finding another publisher willing to continue the story. (In fact, *Barefoot Gen* was ultimately published in three other manga magazines. Every time one would go out of business, another magazine quickly stepped in to continue the series.) In the meantime, Nakazawa found himself

KEIJI NAKAZAWA

Keiji Nakazawa, the manga artist who has served as an unofficial spokesman for the victims of Hiroshima, was born in 1939. He was six years old when the bomb struck the city, killing more than 100,000 citizens.

Nakazawa survived the bombing and aspired to work as an artist. In 1961 he moved to Tokyo, where he found work supplying manga to a number of publications. His early work was typical manga—adventure stories aimed at young male readers. His first successful series, *Spark One*, told of rival race car drivers who bend the rules to get an advantage over one another. In the years that followed he worked on manga stories about baseball players, samurai warriors, and space travelers.

Barefoot Gen established Nakazawa as one of the country's leading manga artists. Over the years Nakazawa has brought Gen back from time to time to remind the world of the horrors of nuclear weapons. In 1995, as the French were preparing to test a nuclear bomb, Nakazawa contributed a single-framed manga to a Japanese publication, showing Gen shouting to the French, "Don't you see that you will be all alone in the world?" Shortly after the North Koreans launched a similar nuclear test in 2006 Nakazawa told a reporter, "I want to say the same thing now."

Quoted in *Mainichi Daily News*, "Fury at the Bomb, the Americans and Japan's Wartime Leaders," October 25, 2006. http://mdn.mainichi-msn.co.jp/features/hibakusha/archive/news/2006/10/20061025p2g00m0fe005000c.html.

much in demand as a speaker before school audiences, peace groups, and similar organizations whose members were eager to hear his story of the bomb's aftermath. "At the peak, I was giving 20, 25 talks a year,"[40] he said.

Clearly, Nakazawa had been instrumental in educating a whole generation of Japanese people about the horrors of the Hiroshima bombing. The anime version of *Barefoot Gen* was released in 1983 and was followed with a sequel, *Rail of the Star*, which was produced three years later. *Rail of the Star* continued the story of Gen three years after the bombing. Since then several other anime producers have released their own versions of the atomic attacks and how they affected the Japanese people. Two films are based on manga written by Nakazawa: *Beneath the Black Rain*, which tells the stories of three female survivors of the attack, and *Fly On, Dreamers!* which relates the exploits of a baseball team composed of Hiroshima orphans. Today, the anniversaries of the bombings of Hiroshima and Nagasaki are treated as national days of mourning in Japan; each city stages ceremonies to remember the victims. What is more, the Japanese media are much more comfortable with reporting news about the ceremonies and commemorative events; documentaries on Hiroshima and Nagasaki as well as other aspects of the war are frequently aired on Japanese TV, particularly in the days preceding the anniversary of the bombings in early August.

Still, there is no question that for years, anime and manga artists largely avoided stories that directly addressed the atomic bomb. Napier has suggested, though, that the Hiroshima and Nagasaki holocausts are a prime motivation for artists who center their science fiction stories in dismal, postapocalyptic times. Images of atomic devastation are prevalent in manga and anime, she said, even though the artists often leave it to the imagination of the viewer to figure out how the world ended up in such a mess. "The most obvious reason behind the high incidence of apocalyptic scenarios is the atomic bomb and its horrific aftereffects,"[41] she said.

Environmental Themes

Themes of war and atomic devastation are not the only issues tackled by Japanese anime and manga artists. Anime has a long history promoting preservation of the environment, dating back to the 1960s when *Kimba the White Lion* aired on U.S. television. The series told the story of a heroic lion cub who defended his African homeland against hunters, trappers, poachers, and other humans who aimed to destroy the animals of the jungle. In later years anime producers continued the theme of environmental protection in such films as *Nausicaa of the Valley of Wind* and *Castle in the Sky*. Both films were produced by Miyazaki, the director of *Spirited Away*, whose environmental activism is well known in anime circles. In *Nausicaa of the Valley of the Wind*, which was produced in 1984, a young princess named Nausicaa must protect her home, the Valley of the Wind, from a sea of pollution that threatens to engulf it. And in *Castle in the Sky*, which was filmed two years later, a magical floating city known as Laputa is saved from destruction. At the end of the story it is revealed that the city is held aloft by a tree, which has sheltered many creatures from the corruption and greed of the humans who populate Laputa. And Miyazaki's other major work, *Princess Mononoke*, tells the story of a struggle by animals against the iron miners who threaten to wipe out their forest.

Environmental messages started making their way into anime and manga as Japan shook off the devastation of World War II and returned to a society of prosperity. The country underwent a construction boom, which meant forests and other pristine areas were leveled to make way for new buildings. Said Toshio Suzuki, a coproducer of *Spirited Away*,

> As we were trying to improve the economy, people worked hard to improve their living standards—but that caused much damage to our environment. Traditionally,

Hayao Miyazaki's film *Castle in the Sky* is one of several anime movies that explores themes involving human greed and environmental destruction.

THE ROBOTS OF JAPAN

The Japanese are fascinated by robots—and not necessarily the type of machines that work on assembly lines in car factories. Many Japanese companies, including Sony, an electronics firm, as well as car manufacturers Mitsubishi and Honda, have conducted research into developing robots that walk on two feet and use their eyes to see and hands to manipulate objects. Propelling this interest in so-called biped robots is a very real social concern: With a declining population, the Japanese are concerned that in the future there may not be enough people to perform manual labor, so they hope to develop robots to do the heavy work.

Of course, dedicated anime fans are well aware of Japan's fascination with robots, dating back to the days when *Astro Boy, 8 Man,* and *Gigantor* hit the airwaves. Today, robots dominate Japanese anime in the *Mazinkaiser, Gundam Seed,* and *RahXephon* series. Said British journalist John Gosling, "It is perhaps significant that Japan is the only country in the world seriously interested in bipedal robot research, and when you look at the walking, talking, running and leaping robots of anime, you can perhaps understand why. There may never be such machines in reality, but don't tell the Japanese that."

John Gosling, "The Hidden World of Anime," *Animation World,* August 1996. www.awn.com/mag/issue1.5/articles/goslingcult1.5html.

in Japan, we were making stories about how the evil men who stole or killed would be punished by the good. We were in a social situation where the bad were destroying our environment, so it was natural for us to depict that in our films. [42]

Even science-fictional anime have included social themes, providing the stories with something more than just plots about rocket ships and heroes seeking to avenge wrongs committed by interstellar villains. Anime science fiction has questioned whether the high-tech gadgetry and environments featured in the stories are good for the human soul. A prime example of a socially conscious science fiction story is *Galaxy Express 999*, which appeared as a manga series and then was adapted into an anime series on TV in 1978. Later, the series' producers developed a feature film and sequel.

Galaxy Express 999 told of the quest of a boy named Tetsuro Hoshino (in a dubbed English version the boy's name was changed to Joey Smith) who sought to avenge the murder of his mother by obtaining a suit that would make him virtually indestructible. As Tetsuro and his guardian, a beautiful and mysterious woman named Maetel, search for the suit aboard an intergalactic train known as Galaxy Express 999 they encounter many adventures as they help the poor fend off their oppressors.

The key theme of *Galaxy Express 999*, though, is the social order that rules the universe: The very rich and powerful have given up their flesh and bones and have had their brains transferred into metal bodies while the poor and unfortunate must stumble through life in their highly vulnerable human bodies. Therefore, each episode deals with the fundamental question of whether technology has gotten out of control—a theme that would later be explored in such American movies as *The Matrix* and *Terminator* and their sequels. A final and quite subtle message about the importance of living in a low-tech world can be found in the design of *Galaxy Express 999*: As they travel from planet to planet, Tetsuro and Maetel ride in a train that resembles an old steam locomotive.

Bringing Two Cultures Together

American anime fans may not realize it, but each time they sit in a theater to watch an anime feature or tune in to an anime series on TV they reward themselves with a strong dose of Japanese culture. Often that experience begins as soon as the images of the characters first flash onto the screen. It also becomes quite apparent as the music on the film's sound track rises in the background.

In American films—whether they are live-action or animated— the background music plays a very important role in telling the story. Typically, a suspenseful scene is punctuated by a growing orchestration in the background. The dramatic entrance of the music and its rise in tempo and volume signals the viewer that something creepy is about to happen.

In anime viewers may hear a totally different orchestration in the background. The sounds made by simple wooden rhythm instruments, like those used in Japan's Kabuki and Noh theaters— performing arts that date back to the fourteenth century—may be employed to create the suspenseful effect in anime. Other sounds familiar to Japanese ears are similarly employed to set the tone for a scene. Price recalled watching one anime feature in which a Japanese insect known as the *semi* chattered away in the background while the camera held steady on a scene of pastoral beauty. Only the Japanese know that the semi comes out on the hottest and most humid days, and that by using the sound of the semi the animator did not need to use any other technique to convey the sweltering temperatures intended for the scene. She said,

A funny thing about anime: no matter how popular it is in the West and how universal it might be, there is no way to disguise its very "Japaneseness." Anime is deeply embedded in all aspects of Japanese society: folklore, legends, history, religion, moral assumptions, and aesthetic standards, to name a few. Fans around the world might be surprised to know that anime is created with only the Japanese audience in mind. . . . The fact that anime has become so popular outside of Japan is quite a mystery to many Japanese animators."[43]

As anime and manga have grown in popularity outside Japan, Japanese artists have not felt the need to alter their work so that it may have a wider appeal to international audiences. On the other

Instruments used in Japan's ancient theater traditions, such as this *shamisen,* often provide haunting background music in anime films.

hand, entertainment executives in America and elsewhere have long ago given up the notion that the Japanese productions must be edited for Western consumption. Gone are the days of samurai-style editing that sanitized most remnants of Japanese culture from *Astro Boy*. Now—with the notable exception of a dubbed English translation—the story that was inked by an artist in Japan is the story that Americans see on their TV or movie screens. It is common now to see anime and manga characters wearing kimonos, eating with chopsticks, and praying to Buddha. Offering anime to American audiences as its animators intended has served a dual purpose: It has maintained the artistic integrity of films, and it has also helped close the gap between two very diverse cultures.

Inspired by Kabuki and Noh

The influences of the ancient Japanese theaters of Kabuki and Noh on anime do not stop with the background music. Even the artistic style of the animators reflects many of the old traditions. Dating back to the days of Tezuka, animators employed the eyes of their characters to convey emotions and move the stories along. Tezuka did this to save money on animation cels, but writers and scholars who have studied anime cannot help but wonder whether Tezuka and the other early animators would have relied on this technique even if they had unlimited budgets. Today, anime artists are still using facial expressions to convey the story, and they also use arms, feet, and other body parts to move the story along as well. Said Gosling,

> Just watch an anime character giving a speech or mono-logue and you will often see that the whole body is used to express his or her sentiments. The character assumes a series of stylized and exaggerated postures, which in spirit echoes the philosophy of the kabuki actor, who from an early age is trained in dance and other techniques to use the entire body as a medium of expression. It seems likely that animators are making a conscious effort to mimic kabuki, but keep in mind that after the Second World War, many kabuki actors made the transition to film and television. Clearly, they would have had to tone

NOH AND KABUKI

The theatrical genres known as Noh and Kabuki have inspired many anime artists. Both forms of theater feature ornate costumes and rituals that have remained unchanged since actors first took the stage centuries ago.

In Noh, which was first performed in the fourteenth century, the dramas typically portray the stories of gods, spirits, or great warriors from Japan's history. Noh actors wear ornately colored costumes and masks and perform under roofed stages. One of the traditions of Noh requires the performers to rehearse separately under the guidance of a teacher. The actors never take the stage together until the actual performance, which ensures a measure of spontaneity in the dramatization.

Kabuki dates back to the seventeenth century and was originally a form of dance performed by female entertainers. Within a few years men took over the roles, and now Kabuki theater is a male-dominated art form. As in Noh, Kabuki actors perform in ornate costumes, but they wear makeup instead of masks. Most kabuki stories relate famous acts of heroism or sacrifice in Japanese history. Unlike most plays, which may run for two or three hours, Kabuki performances can go on all day. Theatergoers often do not endure the whole play but take a few hours from their day to sit in on part of the performance.

down their performances, but I suspect that enough of the essence of their art leaked through to influence the early pioneers in television and film animation. [44]

Indeed, Gosling suggested that anyone familiar with Kabuki theater can see Kabuki movements in anime. For example, most animators open their films and TV episodes with still portraits of their characters—particularly in anime that feature ensemble casts with many characters. Clearly, Gosling said, the poses struck by the characters in the introductory still frames are modeled after the *mie* and *kimari* poses—the most dramatic moments in Kabuki theater when the character draws a sword or clutches a fan and stands rock-still so that the audience can soak in the meaning of the moment. (Mie poses are struck by male characters; kimari poses are assumed by females.)

Meanwhile, in Noh theater it is common for characters to huddle together on the side of the stage and perform a little skit that has nothing to do with the main story that is unfolding on center stage. Gosling said that is a common technique used in anime as well, usually added to the stories for comic relief purposes. Still, he cannot help but wonder whether Japanese animators got the idea for these little comedic asides from productions of Noh theater.

A contemporary Kabuki actor performs. Kabuki theater, with its distinct movements and poses, has inspired many anime artists.

Subtle Influences

Some examples of Japanese culture found in anime and manga are far more subtle than the Kabuki poses and Noh skits, and one would almost certainly have to be very familiar with Japanese culture to recognize them. Still, they are depicted on the screen or in the pages of manga, and through some careful observation they can be recognized.

For example, when the story takes characters into the traditional Japanese rock garden, known as a Zen garden, chances are the plot is about to take a significant turn. In Japanese culture the Zen garden is regarded as a place of tranquillity and national unity. Scholars have interpreted the rocks in a Zen garden as the mother tiger caring for her cubs or the islands of Japan forming a nation. Certainly, when anime characters gather in a Zen garden they are likely to have more than just a casual conversation. During *Spirited Away*, some of the most touching scenes in

A Zen garden in Kyoto presents a tranquil setting in real life, but in an anime film it signals an important change in the direction of the plot.

which the main character, Chihiro, learns about love and friendship are depicted in a beautiful rock garden—particularly the scene where she befriends a hideous monster known as No Face.

Cherry blossoms also have a special meaning in Japan—they bloom in spring but they also portend death. Said Price, "The cherry blossom only blooms for about three days out of the year. It is this impermanence that makes it so highly regarded and symbolic in Japanese culture. So when you're watching anime and you see cherry blossoms falling, it most likely means that someone of great beauty (inside or out) is not going to live on this Earth for much longer."[45]

Likewise, a nosebleed has a meaning to the Japanese that most Americans could hardly be expected to recognize. In Japan, when a boy's nose starts bleeding, it is said that he has become smitten by a pretty girl. Some animators have added their own twists to this quirky little slice of Japanese culture. In the manga and anime adventures titled *Mobile Police Patlabor*, which relate the exploits of a futuristic robot police force, one of the trigger-happy cops suffers from a nosebleed whenever he sees a particularly big gun.

New Rules of Myth

Japanese-style storytelling is woven into anime and manga in more ways than just how the characters are posed, whether they find love in gardens, or their noses bleed at the sight of a big gun or pretty girl. Indeed, one of the characteristics that sets anime and manga apart from not only their American counterparts but from just about any form of fantasy fiction in Western literature is that the Japanese often do not adhere to the standards of myth that have been followed by generations of storytellers.

There are, in fact, definite rules of myth that have been followed by Western authors and storytellers for ages. These rules were established by the ancient Greeks, who spun stories about winged horses, witches with snakes growing from their heads, fierce creatures that were half man and half bull, and one-eyed giants who terrorized shipwrecked sailors. Today these rules are still followed by writers and filmmakers and can be found in such diverse stories as *The Lord of the Rings* and *The Wizard of Oz*.

*A*nime may follow strict cultural lines in Japan, but some Americans have managed to carve out careers in the craft. One American who made the transition is Michael Arias, a Los Angeles filmmaker who has lived about half his life in Japan.

Arias is well known in technical circles in the film business in both Hollywood and Tokyo. He has helped develop the special effects for a number of live-action films, including director James Cameron's horror story, *The Abyss*. In the mid-1990s he developed some computer animation techniques that director Hayao Miyazaki employed in *Princess Mononoke*.

In 2003 Arias became the first American selected to direct an anime film when he took over production of *Tekkon Kinkreet*, which was adapted from a science fiction manga series that related the story of street gangs, mobsters, and greedy developers in the mythical city of Treasure Town. The film was released in 2006 to critical acceptance in Japan. One Japanese film critic, Ryusuke Hikawa, said, "The American director described Japanese emotions and atmosphere very well. . . . Scenes of old Tokyo and people's manners were well depicted and exactly fit the emotions of the Japanese. Of course, the director had good Japanese staff members around. But even so, I wonder how he did it so well."

Quoted in Bruce Wallace, "An American Anime Film?" *Los Angeles Times*, February 4, 2007. www.latimes.com/entertainment/la-ca-arias4feb04,1,4706045.story?ctrack=1&cset=true.

These are two vastly different stories, yet they follow the same familiar rules of myth. The stories begin with the introduction of the hero or heroine and the call to adventure. Next, the reader is introduced to a character who is wiser and serves as a mentor. In *The Lord of the Rings*, the wizard Gandalf advises Frodo the Hobbit; in *The Wizard of Oz*, Glinda the good witch guides Dorothy. Next, the hero begins a journey and along the way enlists friends and allies to go along to provide help. (Aragorn, Legolas, and Gimli in *The Lord of the Rings*; the Lion, Scarecrow, and Tin Woodsman in *The Wizard of Oz*.) There will be many tests and ordeals along the way, which the central characters endure and overcome. The hero or heroine may even suffer through a period of self-doubt and introspection, but in the end he or she resolves to go on. Finally, the journey ends with a confrontation against the villain. In *Lord of the Rings*, Sauron is defeated, and Frodo destroys the ring; in *Wizard of Oz*, Dorothy captures the broom from the Wicked Witch of the West, melts her with a bucket of water, and uses the ruby slippers to return to Kansas.

The rules of myth in Western storytelling have been explored by many writers, most notably American author Joseph Campbell

Like many stories written by authors in the West, *The Lord of the Rings* follows well-established Western traditions of storytelling.

in his 1949 book, *The Hero with a Thousand Faces*. Said Campbell, "A hero ventures forth from the world of the common day into a region of supernatural wonder: fabulous forces are there encountered and a decisive victory is won: the hero comes back from this mysterious adventure with the power to bestow boons on his fellow man."[46]

But anime and manga often do not follow those rules of myth. In Japanese storytelling the hero may have a dark side. Sometimes the hero may not survive the story—he or she will be killed off

MANGA SCHOOL

Manga and anime have grown into a $5 billion-a-year industry in Japan, but until recently most artists were self-taught or graduates of general art programs at Japanese universities. In 2000, though, Kyoto Seika University in the city of Kyoto established a manga program. Currently, some two hundred students are enrolled. Meanwhile, another twenty Japanese universities have also established manga drawing programs.

Kyoto Seika graduated its first class of manga artists in 2004, and about 10 percent have become professional manga artists while the other students have found art-related jobs in other media, such as advertising. Kyoto Seika educators believe that was a good start for a new program and, in time, the percentage of graduates working in manga will rise.

Keiichi Makino, the dean of the university's art school, said Kyoto Seika's program has helped legitimize the profession, which has often been held in low esteem by college professors as well as other Japanese artists. But in the brief time the school has offered the program, Makino said, it has clearly helped some manga artists get their starts. "We went out on a limb," he said. "We had doubts about the viability of teaching in a university setting, especially since a lot of academics considered manga 'trashy.'"

Quoted in "Mad About Manga," *Chronicle of Higher Education*, July 28, 2006, p. A-31.

before the end. The villain may be misunderstood. When the villain dies, he or she may invoke sympathy from the audience. According to Price, the Japanese have adapted the fantastic and mythological stories of manga and anime to life in the real world. Indeed, in the real world the good guys do not always win, and the bad guys may not always be so bad after all.

In *Princess Mononoke*, there is no question that Mononoke is the heroine and Lady Eboshi the villain. And yet Mononoke is often portrayed as a cold-blooded huntress while Lady Eboshi emerges as a sympathetic character. (She gives comfort to lepers and other outcasts.) In the inevitable final battle, Lady Eboshi loses an arm but survives and returns to Irontown, committed to building a new community that will respect the forest life.

In the mythology portrayed in anime and manga, one trend becomes very clear: Japanese mythology is not very mythological

In *Princess Mononoke*, the princess (pictured) often appears less sympathetic than the film's villain, Lady Eboshi.

after all. The application of real-world values and truths to mythological stories is uniquely Japanese, and whether Americans know it or not when they see these stories unfold before their eyes, they are seeing mythology told from a uniquely Japanese point of view. Said Price,

> Perhaps the most intriguing aspect of Japanese animation to American viewers is its realistic approach to mature, relatable topics and its sincere depiction of human emotion. Fans often comment on how anime's creative storylines are treated with genuine, non–glossed over honesty. Characters don't live happily ever after, bad things happen to good people, and villains go unpunished. The Japanese aesthetic tradition of . . . art just so happens to mirror real life situations. [47]

Meeting of East and West

It would seem that American writers and filmmakers could learn something from the anime and manga artists of Japan. Given the rise in popularity of anime and manga in America, they would probably do well to start taking notes. On the other hand, it is unlikely that anime and manga will ever rise to a status in American culture that they enjoy in Japan, but there is no question that the U.S. fan base has grown in recent years. Americans have come to appreciate the art work, the stories, and the concepts explored in anime and manga.

It is a merger of cultures that some poets and philosophers never believed could happen. Rudyard Kipling, the British author and poet, had this to say about the Orient: "Oh, East is East, and West is West, and never the twain shall meet." [48] Of course, Kipling died in 1936 and probably never had an opportunity to watch anime or read manga. If he were alive today, Kipling may have something far different to say about the differences between the Eastern and Western worlds. In its own way, anime has helped teach its American fans about Japan and played an instrumental role in bringing the two vastly different cultures much closer together.

Notes

Introduction: Anime: A Gift from Japan

1. Shinobu Price, "Cartoons from Another Planet: Japanese Animation as Cross-Cultural Communication," *Journal of American and Comparative Cultures*, Spring 2001, p. 153.
2. Price, "Cartoons from Another Planet," p. 153.

Chapter 1: The Roots of Anime

3. Quoted in Henry (Yoshitaka) Kiyama and Frederik L. Schodt, *The Four Immigrants Manga: A Japanese Experience in San Francisco, 1904–1924*. Berkeley, CA: Stone Bridge, 2005, pp. 7–8.
4. Gilles Poitras, *Anime Essentials*. Berkeley, CA: Stone Bridge, 2005, pp. 16–17.
5. Quoted in Japan Foundation Newsletter, "Interview with Mr. Frederik Schodt: Writer and Manga Scholar," June/July 2005, pp. 1–2.
6. Fred Patten, *Watching Anime, Reading Manga: 25 Years of Essays and Reviews*. Berkeley, CA: Stone Bridge, 2004, p. 271.

Chapter 2: Anime in America

7. Patten, *Watching Anime, Reading Manga*, p. 129.

8. Quoted in Harvey Deneroff, "Fred Ladd: An Interview," *Animation World*, August 1996. www.awn.com/mag/issue1.5/articles/deneroffladd1.5.html.
9. Jonathan Clements and Helen McCarthy, *The Anime Encyclopedia*. Berkeley, CA: Stone Bridge, 2001, p. 374.
10. Patten, *Watching Anime, Reading Manga*, p. 59.
11. Quoted in Patten, *Watching Anime, Reading Manga*, p. 306.
12. Clements and McCarthy, *The Anime Encyclopedia*, p. 9.
13. Janet Maslin, "A Tokyo of the Future in Vibrant Animation," *New York Times*, October 19, 1990, p. C-12.
14. Roger Ebert, "*Spirited Away*," *Chicago Sun-Times*, September 20, 2002. http://rogerebert.suntimes.com/apps/pbcs.dll/article?AID=/20020920/REVIEWS/209200306/1023.
15. Quoted in Grady Hendrix, "Manga's the Right Fit for Majors," *Variety*, May 29, 2006, p. A-8.

Chapter 3: What Makes Anime Different?

16. Christopher Hart, *Anime Mania: How to Draw Characters for Japanese Animation*. New York: Watson-Guptill, 2002, p. 7.
17. Poitras, *Anime Essentials*, p. 60.
18. Poitras, *Anime Essentials*, p. 62.

19. Hart, *Anime Mania*, p. 22.
20. Hart, *Anime Mania*, p. 22.
21. Poitras, Anime Essentials, p. 58.
22. Quoted in Calvin Reid, "Harper-Collins, Tokyopop Ink Manga Deal," *Publishers Weekly*, March 28, 2006. www.publishersweekly.com/article/CA6319467.html.

Chapter 4: The Role of Women in Anime

23. Price, "Cartoons from Another Planet," p. 153.
24. John Gosling, "The Hidden World of Anime," *Animation World*, August 1996. www.awn.com/mag/issue1.5/articles/goslingcult1.5html.
25. Quoted in George Gene Gustines, "For Graphic Novels, a New Frontier: Teenage Girls," *New York Times*, November 25, 2006, p. B-7.
26. Quoted in Vanessa E. Jones, "Girl Power—Young Women Are Driving One of the Hottest Trends in Pop Culture: Japanese Comics," *Boston Globe*, July 28, 2004, p. F-1.
27. Quoted in Jones, "Girl Power," p. F-1.
28. Quoted in Jones, "Girl Power," p. F-1.
29. Poitras, *Anime Essentials*, p. 44.
30. Quoted in Charles Solomon, "Four Mothers of Manga Gain American Fans with Expertise in a Variety of Visual Styles," *New York Times*, November 28, 2006, p. E-5.
31. Quoted in Solomon, "Four Mothers of Manga," p. E-5.
32. Susan J. Napier, *Anime: From Akira to Princess Mononoke*. New York: Palgrave, 2000, p. 55.

Chapter 5: The Messages of Anime

33. Price, "Cartoons from Another Planet," p. 153.
34. Clements and McCarthy, *The Anime Encyclopedia*, pp. 153–54.
35. Roger Ebert, "*Grave of the Fireflies*," *Chicago Sun-Times*, March 19, 2000. http://rogerebert.suntimes.com/apps/pbcs.dll/article?AID=/20000319/REVIEWS08/3190301/1023.
36. Napier, *Anime: From Akira to Princess Mononoke*, p. 166.
37. Quoted in Alan Gleason, "Keiji Nakazawa," *Comics Journal*, no. 256, www.tcj.com/256/i_nakazawa.html.
38. Quoted in Gleason, "Keiji Nakazawa."
39. Quoted in Gleason, "Keiji Nakazawa."
40. Quoted in Gleason, "Keiji Nakazawa."
41. Napier, *Anime: From Akira to Princess Mononoke*, p. 29.
42. Quoted in Lynden Barber, "Anime at the Gates," *Australian*, May 15, 2004.

Chapter 6: Bringing Two Cultures Together

43. Price, "Cartoons from Another Planet," p. 153.
44. Gosling, "The Hidden World of Anime."
45. Price, "Cartoons from Another Planet," p. 153.
46. Quoted in William Indick, "Classical Heroes in Modern Movies: Mythological Patterns of the Superhero," *Journal of Media Psychology*, Fall 2004. www.calstatela.edu/faculty/sfischo/ClassicalHeroes.html.
47. Price, "Cartoons from Another Planet," p. 153.
48. Rudyard Kipling, "The Ballad of East and West." www.bartleby.com/246/1129.html.

For Further Reading

Books

Jonathan Clements and Helen McCarthy, *The Anime Encyclopedia*. Berkeley, CA: Stone Bridge, 2001. Comprehensive overview of anime, giving a history of the craft since Oten Shimokawa produced the first Japanese cartoon in 1917 and capsule reviews of virtually every animated film produced in Japan since then.

Christopher Hart, *Anime Mania: How to Draw Characters for Japanese Animation*. New York: Watson-Guptill, 2002. The American cartoonist and art teacher walks students through the entire process of drawing anime characters, from preliminary pencil sketches to completing the elaborate and colorful portraits of the characters.

David M. Haugen, ed., *Comic Books: Examining Pop Culture*. Detroit, MI: Greenhaven, 2005. Includes the essay by Frederik L. Schodt, "Japanese Manga Invades America," chronicling the growth of manga in the United States.

Susan J. Napier, *Anime: From Akira to Princess Mononoke*. New York: Palgrave, 2000. The University of Texas at Austin professor of Japanese literature looks at some of the underlying themes in anime, such as the portrayal of women and how anime artists have treated themes of war, particularly the bombings of Hiroshima and Nagasaki.

Fred Patten, *Watching Anime, Reading Manga: 25 Years of Essays and Reviews*. Berkeley, CA: Stone Bridge, 2004. A compilation of essays and reviews about manga and anime written by the longtime critic and writer; includes interviews and biographical sketches of a number of important anime figures, including *Astro Boy* creator Osamu Tezuka.

Gilles Poitras, *Anime Essentials*. Berkeley, CA: Stone Bridge, 2005. For the viewer just discovering anime, the author provides a background of the craft and explains why the characters have round eyes, colorful hair, and why so many female characters wear sailor uniforms.

Frederik L. Schodt, *Manga! Manga! The World of Japanese Comics*. Tokyo: Kodansha International, 1986. The longtime American authority on anime and manga provides a thorough history of Japanese comics, showing how the art form rose from the drawing boards of the nineteenth-century political cartoonists to become the multibillion-dollar industry of today.

Periodicals

Richard Corliss, Georgia Harbison, and Jeffrey Ressner, "Amazing Anime," *Time*, November 22, 1999. The anime invasion made the cover of *Time* magazine with this overview of Japanese animation, focusing on such titles as *Pokémon, Sailor*

Moon, and *Princess Mononoke;* includes a time line that traces the growth of anime since the 1950s.

Jane Halsall, "The Anime Revelation," *School Library Journal,* August 2004. The librarian of the McHenry Public Library in Illinois explains how she became an anime addict and how she added anime titles to the shelves of her library.

Charles Solomon, "Four Mothers of Manga Gain American Fans with Expertise in a Variety of Visual Styles," *New York Times,* November 28, 2006. Four female Japanese artists who make up the manga team known as Clamp explain in an interview how they work together to produce some of the most read titles in Japan.

Web Sites

Animation World (www.awn.com/mag/issue 1.5/articles/deneroffladd1.5.html). The August 1996 edition of the magazine *Animation World* is available online; the issue was devoted to anime and includes an interview with American *Astro Boy* producer Fred Ladd, a brief history of anime written by Fred Patten, and an analysis of the cultural content of anime by British journalist John Gosling.

Anime News Network (www.animenews network.com). The Web site managed by anime devotees reports the latest developments in the anime industry; corre-spondents in Japan provide news updates while writers in the United States, Canada, and other countries contribute reviews of the latest anime releases. There are also online forums to discuss anime as well as a search engine to retrieve past articles published online by the network.

Kyoto International Manga Museum (www. kyotomm.com/english/about_6.html). Visitors can take a virtual tour of the museum that has been devoted to displaying the best of manga. The museum's Web site includes images of manga dating back to the 1870s; in addition, covers of *Tokyo Puck,* drawn by manga pioneer Rakuten Kitazawa, are on display.

Kyoto Seika University (www.kyoto-seika.ac.jp/eng/3_art/manga.htm). Students who aspire to study manga in the birthplace of the art form can find information on the university's program at this Web site, which provides, in English, an overview of the program, descriptions of the courses, and requirements for admission.

Studio Ghibli (www.onlineghibli.com). Web site maintained by the studio that has produced *Spirited Away, Princess Mononoke, Grave of the Fireflies,* and other top anime films. Visitors can find production details on more than twenty Ghibli films, reviews by critics, still photos, and synopses of the plots.

Index

Picture Credits

About the Author

Hal Marcovitz has written nearly one hundred books for young readers. His other books in the Eye on Art series include *Surrealism*, *Computer Animation*, and *Art Conservation*. He lives in Chalfont, Pennsylvania, with his wife Gail and daughters Michelle and Ashley.